MARCO ⊕ POLO

Tips

ISTANBUL

BULGARIA · Black Sea

MK

○ **Istanbul**

Ankara ○

Izmir ○ **T U R K E Y**

Greece

Antalya ○

Crete (GR)

Cyprus

SYRIA

LEBANON

Mediterranean Sea

ISRAEL

EGYPT

www.marco-polo.com

The best Insider Tips → p. 4

INSIDER TIP

Best of ... → p. 6

Sightseeing → p. 26

Food & drink → p. 60

SYMBOLS

INSIDER TIP	Insider Tip
★	Highlight
●●●●	Best of ...
ゝ゚	Scenic view
☺	Responsible travel: for ecological or fair trade aspects
(*)	Telephone numbers that are not toll-free

PRICE CATEGORIES HOTELS

Expensive	over 130 pounds
Moderate	70–130 pounds
Budget	under 70 pounds

Prices are for two persons in a double room with breakfast per night

PRICE CATEGORIES RESTAURANTS

Expensive	over 34 pounds
Moderate	17–34 pounds
Budget	under 17 pounds

Prices are for a meal with soup, main course, dessert and a drink

On the cover: İstiklal Caddesi, a showcase street p. 48 | Kuzguncuk, a multicultural quarter p. 53

CONTENTS

Shopping → p. 72

Entertainment → p. 80

Where to stay → p. 88

Street atlas → p. 120

DID YOU KNOW?
Football → p. 23
Keep fit! → p. 50
Relax & chill out → p. 57
Gourmet restaurants → p. 64
Local specialities → p. 68
Luxury hotels → p. 92
Budgeting → p. 110
Weather in İstanbul → p. 111
Books & films → p. 112
Currency converter → p. 113

MAPS IN THE GUIDEBOOK
(122 A1) Page numbers and
coordinates refer to the street
atlas and the map of İstanbul
and its surroundings
(0) Site/address located off
the map
Coordinates are also given for
places that are not marked
on the street atlas
Refer to the back flap for a
map of rail transport routes

**INSIDE BACK COVER:
PULL-OUT MAP →**

PULL-OUT MAP 🗺
(🗺 A–B 2–3) Refers to the
removable pull-out map and
the extra map on the pull-out
map

The best MARCO POLO Insider Tips

Our top 15 Insider Tips

INSIDER TIP **Patchwork kelims**
Throw nothing away – that's the motto at Ethnicon. This company's beautiful kelims are unique products, made by joining old fabrics together → p. 79

INSIDER TIP **Swinging İstanbul**
The International Jazz Festival is a highlight of the annual calendar of events. Concerts by high-calibre artists draw crowds at venues scattered across the city → p. 105

INSIDER TIP **A quiet harbour tavern**
Karaköy Lokantasi at the passenger ferry terminal is a good address: the food is tasty and plentiful, the atmosphere is quiet and laid back, and the prices are reasonable → p. 71

INSIDER TIP **Turkish pop and rock**
Club Babylon (photo left) is a rendezvous for İstanbul's alternative music scene → p. 85

INSIDER TIP **A shop for discerning punters**
Haremlique stands for top quality: whether you want items for your bathroom or bedroom, you get the best. The name for this fabric store comes from the women's quarters at Ottoman palaces → p. 79

INSIDER TIP **Hands-on technology**
Stride onto the captain's bridge, visit a submarine or a railway, or admire many other exhibits on the themes of transport, communication and astronomy at the excellent Rahmi-Koç Industrial Museum in Hasköy → p. 103

INSIDER TIP **The history of women's rights**
A wonderful historic building on the Golden Horn is home to an institution that is unique in Turkey: a women's library devoted to the struggle for female emancipation → p. 98

BEST OF ...

GREAT PLACES FOR FREE
Discover new places and save money

FOR FREE

● *Holy places of Islam*
The *Eyüp Mosque* is a major place of pilgrimage, as the Prophet Mohammed's standard-bearer is buried here, and the site therefore attracts the faithful in great numbers. You can visit the mosque free of charge and get in tune with the respectful mood of the pilgrims → p. 39

● *A lively village by the sea*
If you want to sit in comfort on the Bosphorus to enjoy the sunshine and all the goings-on around, you can go to one of the expensive restaurants by the shore. Or save money by taking a trip to *Ortaköy*. There is always something to watch here – from the concentrated backgammon players to the giant tankers on the water → p. 57

● *The seat of the Greek Orthodox patriarch*
A good place to track down the spirit of old Byzantium: the *Church of the Patriarch* in Fener was closed to the public for many years. Now you can visit it free of charge → p. 97

● *Is there an avant-garde artist in the house?*
SALT is the place to go in İstanbul's art scene. Its varied exhibitions give visitors an opportunity to enter into a close dialogue with avant-garde works – free of charge, thanks to the generosity of wealthy sponsors → p. 49

● *In the sultan's garden*
Follow in the sultan's footsteps in *Yıldız Park*. Ancient plane trees create an atmosphere of calm and provide shade. What was once the ruler's private park is now freely accessible to all (photo) → p. 51

● *Tour of the city by tram*
A trip with a tour bus is not all that cheap. By contrast it costs practically nothing to travel round İstanbul by *tram*. The trip from Aksaray to Kabataş, through the old quarter and across the Golden Horn, will set you back just a couple of TL → p. 39

◐◐◐◐ Dots in guidebook refer to 'Best of ...' tips

ONLY IN İSTANBUL
Unique experiences

● *A stroll through the bazaar*
Shopping as in bygone days – at the *Grand Bazaar* you get to know the original oriental version of the shopping centre in its purest form, especially if you take a stroll through its lanes out of season → p. 40

● *A wonderful mosque*
It is one of the largest and most beautiful places of worship in the entire Islamic world: the Sultan Ahmet Camii. Why is it known as the *Blue Mosque*? The question is answered when you enter and see the interior, lined with blue faience (photo) → p. 30

● *Palace of tents*
The *Topkapı Palace* is still a reminder of the way of life of the Turkish people before they arrived in Anatolia. The diverse pavilions that make up the sultan's palace give an impression of tents of stone, even if they are somewhat larger and more opulent than those of the sultan's ancestors → p. 34

● *A boulevard for pleasure and culture*
Sooner or later every visitor to İstanbul ends up on *İstiklal Caddesi*. There is a palpable sense that this fine avenue in the in-district of Beyoğlu is the vibrant heart of the city. Cinemas, bars and culture – there is something here for every taste → p. 48

● *Bridge between contrasts*
The *Galata Bridge* across the Golden Horn is the symbolic centre of İstanbul. Nowhere is the contrast of old and new, oriental and western, as apparent as here. And all the anglers are the clearest possible proof of the importance of the sea as the basis for the existence and life of the city → p. 40

● *Ferry across the Bosphorus*
A *boat ride across the Bosphorus* is one of the most enjoyable experiences in İstanbul. Get aboard in Eminönü and savour the slow trip through the straits to the terminal. Then take ample refreshment in one of the fish restaurants before taking the ferry back. The excursion will give you completely new impressions of the city, and provide some memorable photos of your time in İstanbul → p. 56

ONLY IN

BEST OF ...

RAIN

● **Modern art**
A rainy day is a good opportunity to take a look at the *İstanbul Modern*. Here you can see works by contemporary Turkish painters, sculptors and photographers up close → p. 48

● **Down to the cistern**
When things above ground don't look too sunny, why not dive below the surface? The *Yerebatan Cistern* is a trip back in time (photo) → p. 36

● **Watch football indoors**
In İstanbul watching football in a pub is a week-end ritual that fans practise with Mediterranean enthusiasm. Join in and shout 'goal!' with the locals while eating fish and drinking beer in the *Çarşı Rakı Balık* restaurant → p. 67

● **Istanblues beneath plane trees on the shore of the Bosphorus**
To get a sense of the feeling of melancholy *(hüzün) in* İstanbul that Orhan Pamuk's books conjure up so effectively, take a seat beneath one of the big plane trees on the *Promenade* in Beylerbeyi on a day of non-stop drizzle, and let the scenery take hold of your mood. This never fails to work → p. 56

● **A chic shopping centre**
The *Kanyon* shopping centre is easy to reach by subway even in İstanbul's chaotic rainy-day traffic. You can spend several pleasant hours in the attractive cafés, restaurants, a multiplex cinema and dozens of shops → p. 78

● **Linger in a mystic tea garden**
In the tea garden in the courtyard of the *Çorlulu Ali Paşa Medresesi* time seems to have stood still – especially when the rain patters down. You can sit here for hours and meditate on the impressions you gained in Istanbul → p. 62

RELAX AND CHILL OUT
Take it easy and spoil yourself

● *In a Turkish bath*

Although, or perhaps because, İstanbul is a famously dynamic and bustling city, there are traditional places for relaxation: hamams, Turkish bathhouses. Treat yourself to a soothing massage in the historic *Galatasaray Hamami* (photo) → **p. 57**

● *A carriage ride over the Princes' Islands*

The only traffic sounds that you'll hear are bicycle bells and the clip-clop of hooves – the Princes' Islands are a car-free zone. Hire a horse and carriage to see the main island, *Büyükada,* and leave the sound and fury of the city far behind → **p. 58**

● *A quiet read in green surroundings*

The *Limonlu Bahçe* café is an oasis of peace in the centre of the city and just the spot to do some quiet reading. Get your holiday books out of your bag and order a refreshing mint drink → **p. 63**

● *Tea and a tiptoe through the tulips*

Emirgan Park is Istanbul's loveliest tulip park. Sip a cup of tea from the samovar in the tea house on the Bosphorus and lean back in your seat – no-one minds if you linger here. Afterwards take a relaxing stroll among the flower gardens → **p. 57**

● *Summer festival of classical music*

In the courtyard of the Topkapı Palace, where sultans once took their pleasure, today you can listen to classical music at the *International Music Festival*. After a day filled with new impressions, lull yourself into dreams here on a balmy summer night → **p. 105**

● *A drink at a luxury hotel*

If you'd like to get the feeling of being a guest of state in İstanbul, then indulge in a few of the delightful cocktails in the *Summer Lounge*, the terrace bar of the Çırağan Palace Kempinski luxury hotel. With a view of the Bosphorus, this is a great spot for chilling out → **p. 92**

INTRODUCTION

DISCOVER İSTANBUL

If you have the good fortune to find yourself sitting on a roof terrace above the Bosphorus early in the evening, İstanbul treats you to a unique spectacle: the sun sinks slowly into the Golden Horn, which glistens in the light and fully lives up to its name. The silhouettes of Hagia Sophia, the Blue Mosque and the old palace of the sultans dissolve their contours as darkness falls and ocean-going ships steam from the Sea of Marmara into the Bosphorus. On all sides the muezzins' calls to prayer resound across the roofs. Every famous city leaves you with an unmistakable memory: in İstanbul it is sunsets with an unforgettable backdrop.

At moments like this it is not difficult to gaze with love on İstanbul, this ancient but still beautiful lady on the Bosphorus. And sometimes this frame of mind is necessary in order to overlook the chaotic side of the city. You can easily feel overwhelmed here – for one thing because of the sheer size of İstanbul, for another because the unplanned expansion of the city was for a long time left to the whims of its inhabitants, who now number 13 million. A series of city governments have tried to make

Photo: View past the Dolmabahçe Mosque to the Bosphorus

order out of chaos in recent years, but with limited success. Nevertheless, İstanbul is changing, especially after it was chosen to be one of three European Capitals of Culture in 2010. This event made enough money available for the most significant historic buildings to be restored and given an adequate presentation again. Hagia Sophia, once the largest church in the Christian world, the Topkapı Palace, which was the residence of sultans for centuries, and the great mosques: these world-famous monuments are now once again resplendent. Moreover, the city is becoming more conscious of its history. It no longer ignores its Greek, Byzantine heritage, but puts it on show. Right next to Hagia Sophia archaeologists uncovered the remains of a palace of the Byzantine emperors. The city's oldest harbour was discovered on the Sea of Marmara, at a site on the historic peninsula where delegates from the Greek sea power of Megara founded the settlement of Byzantium in 658 BC, in order to control ships entering and leaving the Black Sea.

> **World-famous monuments have been restored to old glory**

The naming of İstanbul as European Capital of Culture put it up at the top of the list of favourite short city breaks once and for all. The city is a destination for constantly rising numbers of visitors. Cultural globalisation is tangible here. While Arab tourists seek and find western culture, visitors from Europe are fascinated by the city's characteristic mix of the orient and the west: modern shopping malls next to centuries-old

Shopping trip: on the İstiklal boulevard there's always something going on

bazaars, high-rises next to wooden Ottoman buildings, miniskirts and veils – there is no place where the west is as visible in the east as here. Huge contrasts such as that between the thoroughly European district of Beyoğlu and, just a few miles away, the pious Islamic quarter of Fatih are not encountered anywhere else. The ancient Greeks had a word to describe this state of affairs: *paraxenon* – almost alien, but nevertheless still somehow familiar.

One thing is particularly noticeable in İstanbul: the youthfulness of the population. Life is vibrant here, and every visitor feels the dynamism of the city. For visitors from Western Europe, who may have an outdated vision of Turkey

> **Visitors can't fail to notice that the city is buzzing**

as a country that is poor and backward, surprises await: İstanbul symbolises a country that is on the up, and rapidly modernising. Larger than London, Paris or Berlin, the city is home to many wealthy people, and has long been an economic and cultural centre for a whole region that extends far beyond national borders.

It takes no more than the half-hour boat trip from Europe to Asia to get an impression of the variety and breathtaking mix of sights and experiences that is İstanbul. You only have to turn your head a little in order to glimpse the office towers of Levent, a short distance from the impressive oriental scene of the Topkapı Palace, Hagia

Sophia towering above it and a forest of minarets. The first suspension bridge across the Bosphorus is a further sign of the modern world. Only a few miles away from it, the pretty Leander Tower was built into the sea.

The variety of İstanbul's architecture is exceeded by the diversity of its inhabitants. Over the centuries, the tongue of land between the Bosphorus and the Sea of Marmara was taken again and again by conquerors who all put their stamp on it. Greeks and Romans, Persians and Crusaders, Tartars and Turks have left their mark there. Today the descendants of people from all parts of the Ottoman Empire live in İstanbul. In the Byzantine period the Venetians and Genoese had their trading bases. The descendants of Sephardic Jews who were expelled from Spain in 1492 still try to maintain their traditions.

Four out of five residents of İstanbul have come from Anatolia in the last 40 years. In the mid-1960s the city had a population of only 2.5 million. The Asian shore was still largely wooded, and served as pasture for animals or was the site of rural summer dwellings. Today it is every bit as densely populated as the European shore, where the city pushed northwards from the sea. In the meantime the pace of immigration has slowed, and the infrastructure is adapting to the stream of newcomers. The city authorities have ambitious projects designed to put an end to the traffic chaos: a tunnel was built beneath the Bosphorus to take a rail link from Üsküdar on the Asian side to Yenikapı beneath the Topkapı Palace. A further rail link leading to Kartal on the Asian side and new connecting roads round off this scheme. The cable car (finiculère) from Kabataş to Taksim, which has been in operation since 2006, has already calmed İstanbul's traffic.

İstanbul has three city centres today. Sultanahmet, the site of Hagia Sophia and the Blue Mosque with its six minarets reaching for the sky, forms the historic core. As in every other great metropolis that attracts swarms of visitors, this area, including the Topkapı Palace and the Grand Bazaar, is increasingly becoming a tourist zone. Below Sultanahmet, even up to the early 1990s, there were many publishing houses and newspapers that made this district the intellectual heart of Turkey. The second centre, on the western bank of the Bosphorus to the north of the Golden Horn, with its high-rises and upmarket residential areas, has a strongly European character. With Taksim as its heart, it extends from Karaköy to Maslak and has been connected to the subway system. The third important district is the Asian side of the city. The city's most expensive residential areas are located on the Bosphorus and Bagdad Caddesi, which extends above the Sea of Marmara from Kadıköy to Bostancı and many miles beyond.

> **İstanbul has grown around three centres**

Nothing in the history of İstanbul has caused such fear among the city's residents as the earthquake of 1999, a reminder that those who live in this region have to get along with the moods of Mother Earth. Since then projects have been initiated to prepare the city for new tremors and quakes, but the quality of the buildings is very poor in parts, and not everything can be replaced. The catastrophe of March 2011 in Japan showed the people of İstanbul once again how great the danger is. They talk little about this topic. Everyone hopes that the next big quake will come sometime later, preferably in the distant future, and spare their own homes. Compulsory earthquake insurance and stricter new building regulations have been introduced to reduce the future threat.

There's one other way, too, that nature is a dominant force in the life of İstanbul. *Deniz*, the sea, has a direct influence on the city climate. The fishermen are the ones who best know its winds, which can change several times a day. Marine currents alternately carry sea bass and shoals of sardines through the straits. The residents of İstanbul love the northeasterly *poyraz* and detest the *iodos* from the south – the *poyraz* may be a little cool, but the air is so clear that every detail on the opposite bank is visible. When the *iodos* blows, however, it suddenly brings in heat, rain, fog and smog.

> **Deniz, the sea, shapes the climate of the city**

For all the talk about environmental awareness, İstanbul has not really taken this issue to heart. In consequence of the enormous property boom, every available bit of land in the inner city has been built on. Historic quarters are torn down to construct luxury real estate, and green spaces are few and far between in the city centre. Even the woodland at the margins of Istanbul is under threat. Wooded areas that are

A symbol of young İstanbul: students at the entrance to the university in Beyazıt

protected in principle have made way for the guarded, gated communities of the wealthy. For a planned third bridge over the Bosphorus it will be necessary to clear a swathe of woodland to build a motorway. There is, however, resistance to this: committed citizens have formed initiatives to protest against all of these developments.

In the end these matters will be no more than a footnote in the history of a great metropolis. From Byzantium to Constantinople and İstanbul, this city has had more ups and downs than most. And this grande dame has regally dealt with the fact that the founder of the republic, Kemal Atatürk, chose Ankara and not Istanbul to be his centre of power. Its old vitality has returned, and while Ankara may hold the title of capital city, İstanbul has most of the attributes of a true capital. It is the seat of money, the intelligentsia, arts and the media. As the people of the city proudly assert, the best thing about Ankara is the evening flight back to İstanbul.

WHAT'S HOT

1 Cool quarter in the east

Moda Artists and students have discovered the district of Moda, and locations like *Bast Café Kitap (Moda Cad. 245/2)* are definitely hip. Foreign visitors stay at the cool *Hush Hostel Lounge (Rasimpaşa Mah., Rıhtım Cad., İskele Sok. 46, photo)*. From here it's only a short walk to the *Hush Gallery (Caferağa Mah., Miralay Nazım Sok. 20)*. A convenient and authentic way to get to know this quarter is the old-style tram that runs from Kadıköy to Moda *(www.tcdd.gov.tr)*.

Experiments

Bosphorus Fashion The young generation on the Turkish fashion scene has put the burkini, the traditional bathing costume that covers the whole body, firmly behind it and is now taking its place on international catwalks. At the forefront is Selim Baklacı with his futuristic cuts *(shop.selimbaklaci.com, photo)*. The creations of Bahar Korçan are equally eccentric *(Serdar-ı Ekrem Sok. 9)*. The female designer Berra Terzioğlu goes for a glamorous and modern look *(Küçük Bebek Cad. 92)*.

3 New art

On the move Things are really happening in İstanbul's art scene. Galleries like *Pi Artworks* exhibit the works of the wild young generation *(Boğazkesen Cad. 76, www.piartworks.com)*. One of the most coveted exhibition spaces is *Santral*, a former power station covering 118,000 m^2 with galleries, an arts library and a residence for artists *(Kazim Karabekir Cad. 2/6, www.santralistanbul.org, photo)*. To get an impression of what's going on in the scene, go to the annual *Contemporary Istanbul* show *(www.contemporaryistanbul.com)*.

Sleep tastefully

Luxury One-off views, hip designer furnishings and buildings steeped
in history – this is the stuff that hotel dreams are made of. İstanbul
has a whole series of stylish accommodation options
like this. The luxury apartments of the *Galateia
Residence* are one example. Here guests
can choose between apartments varying
in size from 90 to 180 m², every one of
them with spectacular features such
as a view of the Bosphorus, separate
dressing rooms and a concierge service *(www.galateiaresidence.com)*.
Sumahan has found its home in a
former rakı distillery. This chic boutique hotel has a modern interior to
contrast with its historic façade *(Kuleli
Cad. 51, photo)*. For cool design the right
place is the *Witt İstanbul Hotel*, which was
equipped by İstanbul label *Autoban (Defterdar
Yokusu Sok. 26)*.

4

Street food

5

Büfe Bites that are perfect for eating on the hoof:
the countless little snack bars and street stalls –
called *büfe* – are as much a part of İstanbul as
the Blue Mosque. Nevertheless, many tourists
are shy about trying the delicacies that are
on offer here – and they are truly missing
out. The *İstanbul Culinary Institute* has decided to put matters right by organising
tours (photo) on the theme of street food
(www.istanbulculinary.com). The street with
the biggest variety of dishes is İstiklal Caddesi. One of the köfte stalls here has become
a local institution. Thanks to the quality of his
delicious deep-fried meatballs, the owner Ali
Bey succeeded in opening a restaurant: *Sabirtasi
(İstiklal Cad. 112)*, today run by Ali Bey's son.

IN A NUTSHELL

BOSPHORUS

In 1680 an Italian named Ferdinando Marsigli made an important discovery by trailing a plumb line marked with white pieces of cork from a ship in the water of the Bosphorus: first of all the current carried the line westwards. However, at the bottom of the line Marsigli could clearly see that the pieces of cork were drifting in exactly the opposite direction. He had shown that water on the surface of the Bosphorus is flowing from the Black Sea towards the Mediterranean, while in its depths the water flow is going eastwards. This creates treacherous currents and makes a trip through the straits an adventure for captains who have no pilot. The upside is that the water is cleaner here than in any other cosmopolitan city that lies on the sea.

For all the peoples who live on the Black Sea, the Bosphorus is the gateway to the world. As long ago as 658 BC, Greeks founded Byzantium, a settlement established in order to control shipping and collect customs dues. Over the following 2500 years, sovereignty over the 20-mile-long strait was to be the cause of military disputes. It was not until 1936 that the Treaty of Montreux finally regulated the passage of shipping. The people of İstanbul live in constant fear of a tanker accident, which could contaminate the shores of their city. Since 2003 a state-of-the-art radar monitoring system has made the straits safer.

Photo: Scene in a street café

East and west, young and old –
in this city opposites meet to form
a noisy but friendly blend

CONSTANTINOPLE

Constantinople was founded in AD 324 by the Roman emperor Constantine, originally as the 'new Rome' on the site of Byzantium, which had already existed for almost 1000 years. Just before his death the emperor was baptised and made Christianity the state religion. After Constantine it was above all Emperor Justinian (527–65) and his wife Theodora who put their stamp on Constantinople. Justinian commissioned the building of Hagia Sophia, the biggest church in the Christian world, and during the period of the so-called Dark Ages in Western Europe, the most illustrious artists and thinkers of the age gathered in Constantinople. The decline of the Byzantine Empire began in 1071, when its armies lost a decisive battle against the Seljuk Turks at what is today the border between Turkey and Armenia. The final act in this gradual loss of power was played out almost 400 years later: the Ottoman Turks put an end to the weakened Eastern Roman Empire. In

1453 they conquered the city and Constantinople became İstanbul.

ECONOMY

İstanbul is Turkey's financial and business centre. Almost all large Turkish companies have their headquarters there. Support for investment and trade liberalisation have made Turkey an attractive place to do business in the Near East, and İstanbul is the city that benefits most from this.

While the effects of the international banking crisis were felt in Turkey too, they have not taken a heavy toll on the city. As there are no social security systems in place and the Turkish people are used to relying on themselves, there has been no great increase in poverty due to cuts in state spending. This is true despite a high rate of unemployment among graduates and a minimum wage of a mere £ 300. Close family ties substitute government help. However, inequalities of income are extremely marked.

İstanbul's households are enthusiastic consumers, and highly indebted. This results from excessive use of credit cards: everything here, even daily purchases of food, is bought with plastic money and paid off later in instalments.

EU MEMBERSHIP

Turkish politicians have long wanted to strengthen Turkey's ties with Europe, which are especially obvious in İstanbul, by gaining membership of the EU. As long ago as the 1980s Turkey unsuccessfully applied for membership, and since the mid-1990s the country has been a member of the European customs union. In 1999 Turkey was declared to be a candidate for admission, and official negotiations have been under way since 2005. In the years before these negotiations began, the process of convergence with the EU went ahead rapidly, but progress has stalled in recent years. One reason for this is the conflict over Cyprus. Bowing to pressure from Greece, the EU recognised the island as a full member in 2004. Since then Greek Cypriots have blocked the accession talks with Turkey in order to gain concessions from the Turkish inhabitants of Cyprus for reunification. One the other hand the EU states are still at odds over the question of whether they truly want Turkey to be part of the European Union. The conservative French and German governments of Nicolas Sarkozy and Angela Merkel have expressed their reservations. In their opinion, as a predominantly Muslim country Turkey would change the character of the EU too strongly. An alternative mode of cooperation would be a so-called privileged partnership. Although the negotiations have not officially ended, it seems increasingly unlikely that Turkey will be allowed to join the EU.

GENTRIFICATION

This English loan-word, which entered the Turkish language during discussions on urban planning in İstanbul in the middle of the noughties, is used to denote the modernisation of whole quarters, accompanied by the exodus of the old-established, usually poor residents to the outer suburbs. Since the start of the property boom in the late 1990s, the appearance of the city has changed rapidly, especially in the centre. For many years inner-city districts such as Tarlabaşı and Kurtuluş were characterised by immigrants from rural areas of Anatolia who moved into empty older dwellings. However, places that bore signs of decay before the year 2000 found themselves at the centre of a veritable gold-rush mood as prices rose. The

Hagia Sophia still bears witness to the glory of ancient Constantinople

boom has been further fuelled by the fact that the city government has permitted big developers to demolish large areas of old housing and to put new luxury apartments in their place. This is a world away from careful urban renovation; poorer tenants are being pushed out mercilessly. Opposition is growing, however. In many districts citizens' initiatives are protesting against the way residents are forced out of their quarters and against construction on green spaces.

ISLAM

Islam is deeply rooted in Turkey, even though the country is governed as a secular republic. The great majority of the people of İstanbul are Sunni Muslims who observe the five pillars of Islam, including prayer five times daily, fasting during Ramadan and alms for the poor *(zekat)*. For common Friday prayers *(cuma)*, mosques are packed to the doors. The Alevite minority do not go to the mosques but to their own community premises *(cemevi)*, and observe different fasting rules.

From 1923 Kemalist Turks with a western orientation frowned on public religious practice. However, secularisation in the cities did not spread to the countryside. Immigrants from Anatolia became all the more religious as they increasingly found themselves unable to adapt to modern life in İstanbul. An Islamic movement appealed to these troubled voters in the 1980s and eventually came to power in 2002, but moderate Islamists have recently lost some of their support again: voters realised that religion alone cannot provide the answer to social issues. The spread of headscarves nevertheless

Many companies have their headquarters in İstanbul

ered its multicultural heritage. The consequence of the exchange of population with Greece, which was agreed in the Treaty of Lausanne in 1923 and carried out in the following years, was the emigration of 1.25 million Greeks. After the foundation of Israel, thousands of Jews, descendants of Sephardic Jews who were expelled from Spain in 1492, left Turkey in the 1950s. However there were others who stayed: Jewish businessmen such as Ishak Alaton, a manufacturer of electrical goods, and Cem Hakko (Vakko), a fashion designer, are well-known figures in İstanbul today. İstanbul's Armenians were spared the expulsion of 1915, but many of their children emigrated gradually to the west. Today some 60,000 long-established Armenians and about 30,000 who have newly arrived as illegal workers live in the city. These classic minorities have been joined increasingly by Western Europeans who have married Turkish citizens or who come to find work as the city's economy booms. Finally İstanbul is home to several hundred thousand legal and illegal refugees, especially from African countries.

RETURN FROM GERMANY

Almancı, Turks who have returned to their homeland from Germany in growing numbers, are a new phenomenon in İstanbul. Strictly speaking they are not returning, but are the children or grandchildren of immigrants to Germany who were themselves born in Germany and now wish to discover the land of their ancestors. Many of them have a good education and are well integrated in Germany – and nevertheless they are flocking to the Bosphorus. The main reason for this is that there have been attractive jobs in İstanbul for people with this background since the upturn in the new

bears witness to the strengthening of old religious beliefs, especially in the old quarter and in Üsküdar on the Asian side of İstanbul. Two big parallel societies exist: a conservative society and a modern one, which prefer to keep out of each other's way. Bars and clubs can only be found in certain quarters of the city.

MULTICULTURALISM
From the 1990s Turkey rediscov-

millennium. Manufacturing and services are being sourced out of the EU, and a growing number of foreign companies are pleased to take on employees who are at home in both cultures.

Those who 'return' quickly realise how far removed they have become from the homeland of their grandparents. With their western habits and views they run into a wall of prejudice and rejection. Some of them speak Turkish with a German accent. Superficially, their difficulties in integrating are not conspicuous. They quickly learn Turkish and enjoy the material benefits of living in İstanbul, but they remain a largely closed social group within the city. They mainly mix with other returning Turks, as they get along better amongst themselves than with the locals. This situation causes some of them to make a second 'return', back to Germany – or to emigrate to a third country.

SECURITY

Is Turkey a safe holiday destination? Basically yes. Millions of tourists go there every year without giving a thought to the fact that the country still has prob-lems that are expressed in violence. Above all this applies to the unresolved conflict with the Kurdish minority. Since the early 1980s the banned Kurdistan Workers' Party (PKK) has carried out attacks on police stations and army bases with the aim of establishing an independent Kurdish state. These military activities have mainly taken place in southeastern Turkey, though military and civilian targets in Belgium, France and Germany have also been attacked. Foreign visitors to the Mediterranean holiday regions or İstanbul normally notice nothing of this. A subsidiary organisation of the PKK that calls itself the Freedom Hawks (TAK) has also directed operations against tourists in order to cause economic damage to Turkey. These attacks have been rare and isolated incidents. The PKK has repeatedly threatened to carry its war into Turkish cities, but in the end has decided not to do so. It wants to avoid being seen outside Turkey as a purely terrorist organisation. However, to be on the safe side it is worth taking a look at the security warnings issued by your government before you travel.

FOOTBALL

Although Turkish football was rocked by a serious corruption scandal in 2011, it remains the favourite sport of the people of İstanbul. Amongst the teams in the *Süper Lig* there are plenty of ambitious Anatolian clubs joining the three İstanbul clubs Fenerbahçe, Galatasaray and Beşiktaş in the pursuit of trophies. All the same, the championship usually goes to one of the teams from İstanbul, and then all hell breaks loose in the city: millions of fans crowd the broad avenues and squares, gigantic banners are unfurled in prominent places and the club song is played all summer long in every beach disco until most people are tired of it. If you make a trip to İstanbul between October and June, consider joining in the fun and watching the spectacle live. No alcohol is on sale in the stadiums. Tickets are available at *www.biletix.com.tr.*

THE PERFECT DAY

İstanbul in 24 hours

08:30am BREAKFAST IN THE CITY CENTRE

Start the day with breakfast in the centre on *Taksim Square* → p. 50 in the café *Gezi* → p. 62. From here you have a great view of the modern city centre – and a first impression of İstanbul's buzz, and how hectic things are, too.

09:30am A LIVELY AVENUE

Fortified for the day ahead, take a trip on İstanbul's most interesting means of transport, the historic tram system, to ride along *İstiklal Caddesi* → p. 48 (photo left). This way you get to know the upper section of the famous old boulevard with its art galleries, bookshops, cinemas, cafés and shopping arcades. Alight at the Galatasaray Lycée and take a brief stroll through what used to be the flower arcade. The fish market of Beyoğlu will give you a taster of the atmosphere on İstanbul's markets.

10:30am WALK BY THE WATER

From Galatasaray continue on foot along İstiklal Caddesi to Tünel Square, and pay a visit here to the *Mevlevi Monastery* → p. 49, which was once the headquarters of the dancing dervishes in İstanbul. From the monastery a boulevard leads downhill directly to the *Galata Tower* → p. 46. The viewing terrace of the tower gives you a fantastic all-round view of the city centre. After that go down the hill until you are in Karaköy, the heart of the city, by the Golden Horn and the *Galata Bridge* → p. 40.

11:30am A MIDDAY TREAT

The bridge links modern Karaköy with the old quarter. Walking across is a bit like travelling back in time – a feeling that will get even stronger when you plunge into the bustle of the *Egyptian Bazaar* → p. 38 on the other side. This oriental market is a feast for all the senses, as here you will see and smell all the spices you can imagine. Have a good look round to work up an appetite for lunch. *Pandeli* → p. 65 above the entrance to the bazaar is just the job for a good midday meal.

Get to know some of the most dazzling, exciting, and relaxing facets of İstanbul – all on a single day

02:00pm IMPRESSIVE MONUMENTS

On the hill above the spice bazaar stand the two buildings that every visitor to İstanbul has to see: *Hagia Sophia* → p. 32 and the *Blue Mosque* → p. 30. They are among the most impressive places of worship in the whole world. Take time to let these monumental works of architecture work their magic on you.

03:30pm IN THE SULTAN'S PALACE

Beyond Hagia Sophia lies the great gateway to the first courtyard of the *Topkapı Palace* → p. 34 (photo centre), once the residence of the sultan. Explore the extensive palace grounds with their delicate architecture and learn about the long-gone days of the ruling family and their court. After this visit follow the signs to the *Archaeological Museum* → p. 29 and take a break in their tea garden.

06:00pm İSTANBUL FROM THE WATER

Walk through Gülhane Park down to where the boats moor in Eminönü. Private ferry operators offer a two-hour round trip on the Bosphorus. In the light of the setting sun you will see *İstanbul Modern* → p. 48, İstanbul's leading museum of art, and the *Dolmabahçe Palace* → p. 46, before passing under the first Bosphorus bridge and returning to the pier.

08:30pm ROUND OFF THE DAY WITH A MEAL AND MUSIC

Cross the Galata Bridge to get back to Karaköy and take the city's oldest subway line, the *Tünel* funicular railway, back to Tünel Square. In the alleys opposite the exit there are dozens of bars, clubs and restaurants, for example *Yakup 2* → p. 69. If you are still up for it after a meal, drop in at one of the music clubs such as the nearby *Babylon* → p. 85 (photo right).

Starting point: Taksim Square
The historic tram stops behind the Atatürk Monument at the start of İstiklal Caddesi

SIGHTSEEING

CITY **WHERE TO START?**
(129 D2) *(⌂ H5)* **Galata Bridge:** for an exploration of İstanbul's historic old quarter, the Galata Bridge in Eminönü is the best starting point. The main sights in Sultanahmet, İstanbul's museum district, are easily reached from here on foot. You can get to the bridge from anywhere in the city centre by bus, by tram from Kabataş and by ferry from all the main piers on the Bosphorus and on the Sea of Marmara in the southwest. From Taksim you can comfortably walk to the Galata Bridge.

The question of 'now what shall we look at?' is so difficult to answer in İstanbul because the range of different sights is enormous.

In the almost 3000 years of the city's history as the capital of great empires, under the names of 'Byzantium', 'Constantinople' and later 'İstanbul', countless architectural and other monuments were built. Starting with Byzantine remains, which amount to much more than just the world-famous Hagia Sophia, and moving on to 3000 mosques, hundreds of Ottoman palaces, summer residences and forts, Armenian, Greek Orthodox and even Protestant churches, as well as synagogues, you can visit almost everything that touches on the foundations of western civilisation.

Photo: View inside the Süleymaniye Mosque

Ancient Byzantium and the Ottoman Empire: in İstanbul these two empires left a legacy of buildings of unfading beauty

Churches and mosques, palaces and other sights are scattered across the whole city, but there is a concentration of them on the European side. In a city where Byzantine and Islamic traditions banned pictorial representation, there are no venerable galleries of paintings. To make up for that, the private museum market is flourishing: *İstanbul Modern*, a magnificent museum of contemporary art, has been established by the harbour. The *Sabancı Museum* has gained a reputation thanks to spectacu-lar exhibitions, with works by Picasso and Rodin for example and on the subject of Genghis Khan. And the *Pera Museum* is a gem displaying contemporary art and archaeological exhibits.

However, the charm of İstanbul consists not only in its monuments but rather in the existence of different ways of life side by side. The old quarter, where the districts of Fatih and Üsküdar are mainly populated by faithful Muslims, the ar-eas of impoverished immigrants on the Golden Horn and the modern residen-

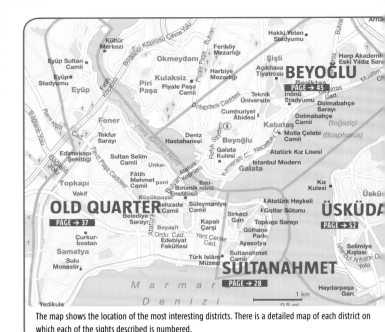

The map shows the location of the most interesting districts. There is a detailed map of each district on which each of the sights described is numbered.

tial districts around Taksim Square are worlds apart.

Don't try to do too much! Monuments such as the Topkapı Palace and Hagia Sophia are worth several hours of your time. Bearing in mind that you have to get from place to place, it is best to decide on a district and then spend the day there on foot. Most major sights such as the palaces and mosques are on the axis of Sultanahmet–Beşiktaş, where a tram connects Beyazıt and the Golden Horn with the Dolmabahçe Palace. İstanbul's buses are best avoided, especially in summer. Taxis are the most comfortable means of transport. City tours are run by *Plantours (Cumhuriyet Caddesi 131/1 | Elmadag | tel. 0212 2 34 77 77 | www.plantours.com)*. The buses leave from opposite Hagia Sophia

(hourly, June–mid-Oct 9am–6pm, mid-Oct–May 9am–4pm | duration 1–2 hours | from £ 15). The municipal bus company also operates round trips for tourists in open-top double-deckers. Starting at Sultanahmet Square the tour costs about £ 13 (at weekends and on public holidays £ 15). You can hop on and off as often as you like on one day.

SULTANAH-MET

Around Sultanahmet Square discover the city's three most famous buildings: the Blue Mosque, Hagia Sophia and the Topkapı Palace.

This is the tourist heart of İstanbul with a magnificent heritage from both the Christian Byzantine period and the Muslim Ottoman period – a must for every visitor to İstanbul. The park at its centre is perfect for taking a break. In summer the mosques and churches are beautifully illuminated at night. The INSIDERTIP tea garden in the sculpture court of the Archaeological Museum directly below the palace is justly regarded as one of the nicest in İstanbul. Round off your visit with a walk through the old *Mint*, where the sultan's currency was coined. Right opposite Hagia Sophia a special treat, especially on hot summer days, involves descending to the huge subterranean *Yerebatan Cistern*. Even children with a museum allergy will find it wonderful. Note: most architectural sights have been converted into museums and are closed on Mondays!

■■ ARCHAEOLOGICAL MUSEUM (ARKEOLOJI MÜZESI) ★
(129 E4) (*Ⅲ J6*)

The main reason for building the Archaeological Museum below the Topkapı Palace was to create worthy surroundings for exhibiting an exceptional find: the *Alexander Sarcophagus*, which Turkish archaeologists found in Sidon, now in Lebanon. It was used to bury not Alexander the Great himself, but a Lebanese king. However, it is an extremely early, uniquely preserved depiction of Alexander. The world-famous sarcophagus dates back to 310 BC, but is completely intact, including its wonderful marble reliefs.

In addition to this showpiece, sarcophaguses from Sidon are on display, and in other rooms sculptures from the Greek, Roman and Byzantine periods. A side wing shows finds from İstanbul's prehistory.

The *Museum of Ancient Oriental Art (Eski Şark Eserleri Müzesi)* in a dedicated build-

MARCO POLO HIGHLIGHTS

ing on the same site has been beautifully designed in a visitor-friendly way and is home to interesting exhibits from ancient Mesopotamia, mainly from the Babylonian and Assyrian periods. The outstanding attraction here is the peace treaty of Kadesh, an agreement written in Hittite cuneiform script that was made in 1259 BC between the Hittite king Hattusili II and the Egyptian pharaoh Ramses II – the oldest surviving document of this kind anywhere.

A third, smaller building on the museum grounds was restored and reopened in 2005. It is the *Faience Museum (Çinili Köşk)*, an exhibition of valuable objects spanning several periods. The art of producing coloured tiles protected by a glaze was highly developed in the Ottoman Empire. The tulip was a popular motif. The dominant colour was azure blue, made to a formula that only a few masters of the craft knew. The *Çinili Köşk*

is the oldest building in the Topkapı Palace. *Tue–Sun 9am–5pm | admission approx. £ 6.50 | Osman Hamdi Bey, Yokuşu | Gülhane, Eminönü | entrance from Gülhane Park*

▣ BLUE MOSQUE (SULTANAHMET CAMII) ★ ● (129 D–E5) (⌀ H7)

At first sight this is the most impressive mosque in the city, its domes rising to the sky in three stages. The Sultanahmet Mosque – to give it its official title – is better known as the Blue Mosque, a name it received thanks to the wonderful blue tiles that adorn the walls inside. It was constructed in the early 17th century at enormous cost to the Ottoman state. However, posterity can be grateful that the money was spent. The outer courts opposite Hagia Sophia are impressive in their dimensions alone. Inside the dominant features, apart from the blue tiles, are the red carpet and the enormous

World-famous tomb: the Alexander Sarcophagus was not however the grave of Alexander the Great

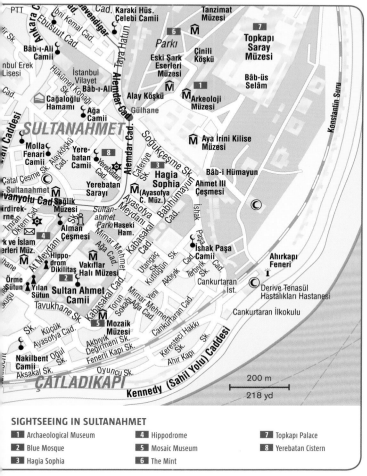

SIGHTSEEING IN SULTANAHMET

1 Archaeological Museum   **4** Hippodrome   **7** Topkapı Palace

2 Blue Mosque   **5** Mosaic Museum   **8** Yerebatan Cistern

3 Hagia Sophia   **6** The Mint

chandeliers that are suspended from the dome. From some of the 260 windows – many of which are glazed with coloured glass – there are views of the Sea of Marmara or a pretty mosque garden.

The so-called sultan's mosques are always accompanied by major charitable foundations. The Blue Mosque too was once surrounded by such a complex (kül-liye), which included a school of theology (medrese), a hospital, a caravanserai and kitchens for the poor. Today only the kitchens remain and the tomb (türbe) of Sultan Ahmet I. On his visit to İstanbul in 2006 Pope Benedict entered the Blue Mosque and meditated there a while. Tourists have access to the mosque through a special entrance, and women who are not Muslim are not required to cover their heads. *Daily 9am–12.30pm, 1.45–4.30pm and 5.30–6.30pm, tomb daily 9.30am–4.30pm | Sultanahmet Meydanı*

▣ HAGIA SOPHIA (AYASOFYA) ★
(129 E4–5) (*⑪ J7*)

Not wanting to sound sacrilegious, but Hagia Sophia, the 'Church of Holy Wisdom', squats above the old quarter of İstanbul like a toad with fat legs and its back arched high. With its glowing red masonry and the four minarets that were added in the Ottoman period, this almost 1500-year-old monument is still one of the characteristic buildings on the skyline of İstanbul and remains an emblem of the city to this day.

What was the largest church in the Christian world in ancient times presents an imposing sight to visitors entering its nave: the massive dome appears not to be heavy, but seems to float at an airy height as if to mirror heaven on earth. A row of 40 windows around the lower part of the dome skilfully illuminates the interior and enhances this impression. The architects resorted to a brilliant trick to create the illusion of a weightless dome: they supported the main dome by means of half-spheres and were thus able to remove to the aisles the buttresses that take the weight of the domes. In this way a gigantic open nave was built. A revolutionary approach for the architecture of the time, this idea was later the model for the construction of mosques in İstanbul and for the Blue Mosque, which stands opposite Hagia Sophia.

The building of Hagia Sophia was commissioned by Emperor Justinian, who was able to dedicate it on 27 December 537 after a sensationally short construction period of just 5 years and 10 months. The structural experiment of building a dome with a diameter of 31 m that floats 160 ft above the ground at its highest

First a church, then a mosque, today a museum: Hagia Sophia and its beautiful garden

point soon proved to have stretched architectural know-how to its limits, however. Several small earthquakes caused it to crack and collapse in 558. When it was rebuilt the external buttresses were reinforced, leading to the squat external appearance of Hagia Sophia, and the dome was raised a further 23 ft to a height of 183 ft. No other Byzantine or Ottoman dome ever attained this height. The interior fittings of Hagia Sophia, which was converted to a museum in 1935, bear the marks of the 500 years when it served as a mosque. Only three days after the conquest of Constantinople in 1453 this imperial church was declared to be the sultan's mosque. In the apse of the church is the *mihrab*, the prayer niche that shows the direction of Mecca. To its right is the *minbar*, the imam's pulpit. The most conspicuous items are large wooden signs, 7.5 m in diameter, at gallery level, bearing calligraphy of the eight most sacred names of

Jesus mosaic in Hagia Sophia

Islam. On closer inspection a number of works of art from the Byzantine period can be made out, especially remains of the famous mosaics. The first of them can be seen in the anterooms to the main building, and the best-known is a 10th-century mosaic directly above the so-called imperial gate. It represents Christ in Majesty. Further mosaics can be seen in the apse and on the walls of the galleries, to which women were confined in both the Byzantine and the Ottoman periods. The most impressive mosaic is a devotional image, a deesis, which depicts Jesus with Mary and John the Baptist.

In the garden of Hagia Sophia are three mausoleums in which sultans Mehmet III, Selim II and Murat III were laid to rest. Around the building the foundations of its predecessor, a 5th-century church, were uncovered in the 1980s. *Tue–Sun 9.30am–4.30pm, gallery 9–10.30am and 1–3pm | admission approx. £ 8*

▣4 HIPPODROME (AT MEYDANI)
(129 D5) (*ᗕ H7*)

The Hippodrome was for Byzantium what the Colosseum was for Rome: the place where the people were kept happy with games and chariot races. This arena is said to have accommodated some 100,000 spectators, but little remains today of the high tiers of the Hippodrome beyond the columns that Constantine caused to be placed on the *spina*, the long platform in the middle of the race-track.

The oldest of them is an Egyptian obelisk that was built in 1900 BC and transported from Luxor to Byzantium. The snake column next to it is said to have come from Delphi. Of the last in the row, the Bronze Column, nothing is known except that it was restored in the 10th century. A fourth column that originally stood here and was crowned by four bronze horses was carried off by the Venetians as spoils of war after the Fourth Crusade.

The paved road around the lawn on which the columns now stand corresponds to the circuit that was used for the races in ancient times. However, the Hippodrome also had a political function: spectators would support either the green or the blue team, an allegiance that corresponded in some periods either to a reforming or a conservative attitude. A dispute between the green and the blue charioteers in 532 led to the Nica rebellion, which Emperor Justinian bloodily suppressed. When it was over, 30,000 corpses are said to have lined the Hippodrome. *At Meydanı*

▣5 MOSAIC MUSEUM (MOZAIK MÜZESI) (129 E5) (*ᗕ H–J7*)

The restored mosaics of the Byzantine imperial palace have been turned into a museum on the original site. The best-preserved floor mosaics depict scenes of hunting and shepherds. *Thu–Tue 9.30am–5pm | admission approx. £ 4 | Kabasakal Cad. (behind Arasta Market)*

▣6 THE MINT (DARPHANE-I AMIRE)
(129 E3) (*ᗕ J7*)

The old mint of 1727 lies below the Topkapı Palace and opposite the Archaeological Museum. It can also be entered from Gülhane Park. Several rooms inform visitors about the production of coins, while other spaces are devoted to temporary exhibitions on the city's history or used for events. The whole complex, including a INSIDER TIP lovely café, is one of the most successful examples of restoration in the city, as it shows how careful refurbishment and a new use can be combined to best advantage. *Wed–Sun 10am–7pm| entrance from the first court of the Topkapı Sarayı or from Gülhane Park | tram from Eminönü in the direction of Beyazıt | www.istanbulmuzesi.org/darphane*

▣7 TOPKAPI PALACE (TOPKAPI SARAYI) ★ ● ᴥ (129 F3–4) (*ᗕ J–K6*)

For more than four centuries the Topkapı Palace was the centre of the Ottoman Empire, a world power. It was the residence of the sultan, the political and religious leader of Muslims, and his harem family. From here the empire was ruled and the top administrators trained, with the sultan's elite corps of soldiers, the Janissaries, based here too. Although the palace grounds are very extensive – at times more than 5000 people lived within its walls – it does not look monumental. All the buildings are single-storey or have two storeys, and are distinguished more by the delicacy of the architecture than by majesty or massiveness – some observers have seen it as a stone version of a village of tents.

Topkapı Sarayı is divided into four courtyards. The first of them, entered through the *Bab-ı Hümayun*, the Imperial Gate, was the base of the Janissaries in the Ottoman period. The church on the left conducted. The cabinet *(divan)* met here, it was the place to wait for an audience, and also the quarters of the executioner, who carried out the sultan's judgments in the first courtyard. On the left, diago-

The Topkapı Palace was the centre of power of the Ottoman Empire

as you enter, the 8th-century *Aya Irini* or Church of Heavenly Peace, was used by soldiers as an arsenal and weapon store. Its unspoiled original appearance makes it one of the most impressive remaining Byzantine places of worship, but the interior is not open to visitors.

At the end of the first courtyard, at the *Bab-ı Selam* or Gate of Peace, the palace museum begins. The second court, which you now enter, was where the business of the Ottoman Empire was nally opposite the entrance gateway, lies the 'divan'. In one corner is a lattice window through which the sultan could keep a clandestine eye on cabinet meetings. On the opposite side of the courtyard is the enormous kitchen wing, where superb meals were prepared for thousands of people. Today it is home to the largest collection of Chinese porcelain outside China. Unfortunately only a fraction of the 10,000 items in the collection are on display.

The second court also gives access to the legendary harem, the sultan's private apartments, which no man other than the sultan himself and his sons was allowed to enter. The sultans kept hundreds of women here. It was the centre of palace intrigues, ruled over by the 'Black Eunuch', the guardian of the harem. The true ruler of the harem, however, was the *Valide Sultan*, the sultan's mother. A tour of the harem takes visitors to luxurious bathrooms, splendid day rooms and a wonderful reception chamber, but also gives an impression of the cramped conditions in which the women here were forced to live. Over 300 rooms were crammed into a space of only 6 700 m². Once every half-hour a small group is permitted to enter the harem. It is recommended to buy tickets immediately and continue visiting the rest of the palace while waiting for the time of entry on the ticket.

The exit leads to the third courtyard, the most important exhibition area in the museum today. Directly behind the gateway to the third courtyard, the *Bab-ı Saadet*, or Gate of Felicity, is the sultan's audience chamber, where the original throne can still be admired. The highlight of a visit are the rooms adjoining the courtyard to the right, where the most beautiful robes, the rarest weapons and the most valuable treasures of the Ottoman Empire are on display. You can see, for example, the famous Topkapı Dagger, feathered helmets inlaid with jewels and the 86-carat Spoonmaker's Diamond. Directly opposite on the other side of the courtyard are religious treasures, including such relics as the proverbial hair from the beard of the Prophet, a footprint left by Mohammed and parts of the gates of the Kaaba in Mecca. Verses from the Koran are recited here during visiting hours. The fourth and last courtyard is not an enclosed space but a large garden in which several pavilions were used by the sultan for rest and recreation. On the right, part of the palace has been converted into a café from which you get a wonderful view of the entrance to the Bosphorus, the Genoese quarter and the Asian part of İstanbul. *Wed–Mon 10am–5pm (ticket sales until 4pm), on the first day of Ramadan and the Feast of Sacrifice midday–4pm, harem 9.30am–3.30pm | admission to Topkapı approx. £ 8, harem and treasury approx. £ 5 each*

■8■ YEREBATAN CISTERN (YEREBATAN SARNICI) ★ ● (129 E4) (*Ø H7*)

Ancient Byzantium was provided with many cisterns to supply the city with water, as there was no natural source of drinking water on the peninsula. The

largest of these cisterns, called the 'sunken palace' by the Turks, lies straight opposite Hagia Sophia and is open to visitors. You descend via a narrow stairway and are suddenly confronted by a huge subterranean space, so large it is impossible to take it all in at once. There is still water in the cistern, but walkways permit you to do a circuit of this fascinating underground world to the sound of classical music. For 1400 years a total of 336 columns have held up the roof. Two of these columns stand on ancient heads of Medusa. In summer INSIDER TIP concerts are held on a platform. There is a café in the entrance area. *Daily 9am–6pm | admission approx. £ 4 | Yerebatan Cad. 7 | www.yerebatan.com*

OLD QUARTER

The 'historic peninsula' was the centre of Constantinople at the time of the Byzantine Empire. This old quarter is bounded on one side by the Sea of Marmara and on the other by the Golden Horn.
It also lies within the enormous, miles-long ancient city wall, which has been restored in parts and encompasses two former Byzantine palaces and the Muslim residential districts. At the heart of the quarter is the Grand Bazaar, the traditional roofed space for traders, where the people of the city once came to buy everything they needed. Next to this centre of commerce is the seat of learning:

The Turks dubbed the impressive Yerebatan Cistern the 'sunken palace'

Nowhere in İstanbul can you see more beautiful Byzantine mosaics than in the Chora Church

the oldest university adjoins the bazaar directly. It is also only a short walk from here to the Süleymaniye Mosque, the most magnificent in all of İstanbul. It is worthwhile venturing deeper into the maze of alleyways for a few hours to immerse yourself in a world which you might think no longer existed.

■1 EGYPTIAN BAZAAR (MISIR ÇARŞISI) (129 D2–3) (*∅ H5*)

The Egyptian Bazaar is also known as the Spice Bazaar, as spices have been the speciality of this market since time immemorial. The dealers pile up their exotic ingredients into colourful heaps. The time-honoured aesthetics of product presentation in the bazaar seem so touchingly out of date in comparison to modern advertising that it's tempting to buy several bags of the colourful spices for that reason alone. If you are looking for dried fruit, all kinds of nuts,

INSIDER TIP healing herbs, caviar or hand-woven baskets, this is the right place. *Mon–Sat 9am–7pm/ Eminönü Meydanı*

■2 CHORA CHURCH (KARIYE CAMII) (122 B3) (*∅ C3*)

This building is neither a church nor a mosque today, but a museum. It contains the finest Byzantine church mosaics that can be seen in İstanbul. The Chora Church, built around 1320, originally belonged to a monastery founded in the 6th century. In its present form it was a donation of Theodoros Metochtites, a Byzantine chancellor who died here as a monk.

In the centuries when the church was used as a mosque, many of the mosaics were covered with wood or painted over. They were only uncovered in the 1950s by the *Byzantine Institute of America*. The mosaics tell three stories: the life of the

Virgin Mary, a cycle of scenes about the youth of Jesus and the story of salvation. The central space of the church also preserves a large portrait of Christ, an image of the Virgin and the scene of the Dormition (death) of Mary. Many of the mosaics are astonishingly well preserved and demonstrate the undiminished artistic prowess of Byzantium in a period when the golden age of the Eastern Roman Empire had long passed.

The Chora Church is part of a larger historic complex that the Turkish Automobile Club has beautifully restored. This area of Ottoman wooden houses is somewhat hidden away close to the city wall at Edirnekapı. Before leaving, treat yourself to a cup of coffee in the lovely INSIDER TIP garden of the Kariye Hotel *(daily 9am–10pm)!* Thu–Tue 9am–4.30pm | admission approx. £ 5.50 | Kariye Camii Sok. | Edirnekapı

■ EYÜP (130 C4) (*Ø 0*)

If you never get to Mecca, you should at least pay a visit to the ● INSIDER TIP Eyüp Mosque. Eyüp is the 'holy quarter' of İstanbul and an important place of pilgrimage for the shrine of Eyüp Ensari, Mohammed's standard-bearer, who lost his life here during the first Arab siege of Constantinople in the 7th century. Immediately after taking the city in 1453, Mehmet II built a great mosque in honour of the martyr and had his bones solemnly buried for the second time. In this way the Ottomans purposefully began to give their new capital city greater weight in the Islamic world. Today the faithful come from all over Turkey to this holy place. Next to the mosque is an extensive cemetery. You can take an attractive walk through the cemetery on a path that leads up the slope. *Bus and ferry from Eminönü*

■ FATIH MOSQUE (FATIH CAMII) (127 F2) (*Ø E5*)

This mosque would be the oldest in İstanbul if it had not been destroyed by an earthquake in 1776 and then rebuilt. The original structure was commissioned in 1463 by Mehmet II only ten years after his conquest of Constantinople, and was intended to be the Muslim answer to the Christians' Hagia Sophia. For that reason the site was carefully chosen. The Fatih Camii was constructed on the ruins of the Church of the Holy Apostles, on the fourth hill of the city, which was the imperial necropolis in the Byzantine period. With this mosque Sultan Mehmet II, known as Fatih ('the Conqueror'), erected a monument to himself. Of the old 15th-century mosque only three porticos of the forecourt, the main gate to the prayer hall and its *mihrab* (prayer niche) survived the earthquake. The mausoleum of the conqueror and his

LOW BUDGET

▶ For 50 pence the *cable car in Eyüp* (130 C4) (*Ø 0*) takes you up over 1800 ft to Café Piyer Loti on the Ottoman cemetery hill, from where you can look out over the Golden Horn. A fantastic trip for a low price! *Oct–June daily 8am–8pm, July–Sept 8am–10pm | entrance on Cami Meydani (Mosque Square)*

▶ Low-budget sightseeing: a leisurely ride on the ● *tram* from Aksaray (128 A4) (*Ø E7*) to Kabataş (125 E2) (*Ø L2*). The token costs less than pound. You pass right through the old quarter and cross the Golden Horn on the Galata Bridge.

More than a transport link: beneath the Galata Bridge a hip scene has arisen

wife Gülbahar stands in the courtyard of the mosque. The mosque and the surrounding complex are the centre of the city district of the same name, which is among the most pious quarters of İstanbul. *Wed–Sun 9.30am–4.30pm | İslambol Cad. | Fatih*

5 GALATA BRIDGE (GALATA KÖPRÜSÜ) ● (124 B6) (*∭ H4–5*)

The Galata Bridge is an emblem of İstanbul. At the mouth of the Golden Horn it connects the old quarter with the modern districts to the north.

The oldest recorded structure to cross the Golden Horn was built in the 6th century AD under Emperor Justinian I. This bridge is said to have consisted of twelve arches. 1000 years later, after the conquest of İstanbul, Sultan Beyazıt II commissioned Leonardo da Vinci to design a new crossing. However da Vinci's plan did not please the sultan and was

shelved. Michelangelo too was personally invited to İstanbul to design a bridge over the Golden Horn, but he never took up the invitation. It was only in the 19th century that Mahmud II built a pontoon bridge, which remained in use until 1912. In the same year a German company built the first modern Galata Bridge on the site of the present one. This steel construction, 466 m long and 25 m wide, was in use until a fire broke out in 1992. Today's bridge is a reconstruction carried out by Turkish companies.

The bridge can be opened at the centre to let tall ships through. In daylight hours countless anglers are to be found here, and many good places to eat nestle under the bridge.

6 GRAND BAZAAR (KAPALI ÇARŞI) ★ ● (128 C4) (*∭ G6*)

The Grand Bazaar forms the heart of the old quarter. Every visitor who passes through one of its 17 gates for the first time will get lost in the labyrinth of alleyways and feel relieved to come across one of the teahouses and take a break there. This ancient shopping mall extends from the Nuruosmaniye Mosque to the Beyazıt Mosque, covering an area of 32,000 m², and sells everything that sets a tourist's pulse racing, from carpets to jewellery and leatherware. A stroll through the bazaar is a delight for all the senses, but you need strong nerves, as tourists are pestered mercilessly. The market has a more authentic feel outside the peak season, when not so many foreign visitors are wandering around there. The bazaar is organised by trade, and every craft has its own 'quarter'. Today the premises are mainly devoted to sales rather than production, even though coppersmiths and tailors can be found at work here and there. Its centre is the *Old Bedesten*, where the numerous antique dealers do business. Construction of this, the oldest part of the bazaar, was ordered by Mehmet II after his conquest

of Constantinople. In the hundred years that followed, the other areas were added one by one. As there are plans to repair the decrepit roof in stages, closures of parts of the bazaar can be expected in the coming years. If you leave the bazaar through one of the gates on the Golden Horn side, you can pass through the traditional quarter of the woodworkers, INSIDER TIP Tahtakale, and stroll down to the sea. This is one of the most authentic shopping areas in İstanbul and is still well frequented by the locals. *Mon–Sat 8.30am–7pm| Beyazıt*

▇7 COLUMN OF CONSTANTINE (ÇEMBERLITAŞ) (129 D4) (*ΩΩ H7*)

The Column of Constantine is the city's oldest monument. It was erected in AD 330 when Byzantium was made the capital city of the Roman Empire and was once the main attraction on the Forum of Constantine. Originally it bore a statue of Emperor Constantine, representing him as the sun god Helios. *Cağaloğlu*

Oriental shopping paradise: you can browse for hours in the Grand Bazaar

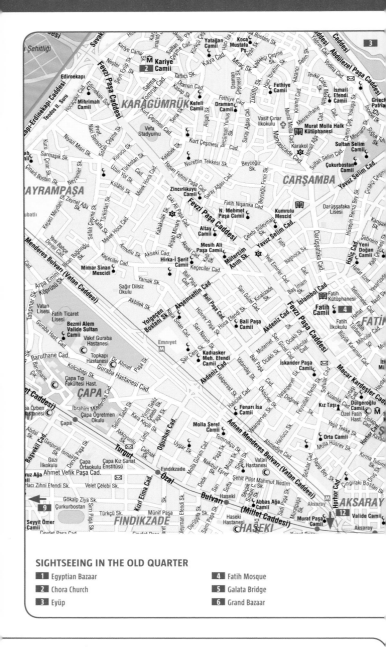

SIGHTSEEING IN THE OLD QUARTER

1 Egyptian Bazaar

2 Chora Church

3 Eyüp

4 Fatih Mosque

5 Galata Bridge

6 Grand Bazaar

7 Column of Constantine
8 Pantocrator Monastery
9 City walls
10 Süleymaniye Mosque
11 Aqueduct of Valens
12 Yedikule

■8■ PANTOCRATOR MONASTERY (MOLLA ZEYREK CAMII)
(123 E6) (*ΩΩ F5*)

This 12th-century monastery was converted to a mosque complex after the conquest of İstanbul. In 2006 it was restored,
a project in which the Turkish architects
were highly successful. The Pantocrator
in fact consists of three churches that
were later combined. The monastery
is thus the best-preserved building of
the Byzantine era after Hagia Sophia.
INSIDER TIP The old quarter around the
building makes a completely unspoilt
impression. *Tue–Sun 9am–5pm | £ 5 |
Sinanağa Mahallesi | Zeyrek, Fatih*

■9■ CITY WALLS (SURLAR)
(126 A–B 1–6) (*ΩΩ A–D 1–8*)

The city walls, built in 412 under Emperor Theodosius II, are so strong that
they were never overcome by siege, and
much of them has survived to this
day. The main wall, 5 m thick and up
to 36 ft high, extended from the Sea of
Marmara to the Golden Horn, giving the
city complete protection from the land-
ward side. To gain the best impression
of this imposing structure, take a walk
from the Yedikule bastion to the Golden
Horn. But don't attempt this if you are
not a seasoned walker, as it is a distance
of four miles!

■10■ SÜLEYMANİYE MOSQUE (SÜLEYMANIYE CAMII)
(128 B–C3) (*ΩΩ G5*)

It may not be as famous as the Blue
Mosque, but those who know their architecture regard the Süleymaniye Mosque
as the city's outstanding religious building. When you look towards the old
quarter from the Galata Tower, you can
see that the Süleymaniye Mosque still
dominates the skyline of İstanbul. It was
designed by the most famous architect of

the Ottoman Empire, Koca Mimar Sinan,
in honour of the most glorious sultan,
Süleyman the Magnificent, between
1550 and 1557.

Thanks mainly to its height, the interior
of the mosque forms an overwhelm-
ing space. The dome is an architectural
masterpiece. Magnificent arcades, incor-
porating columns that are said to have
been taken from the former Byzantine
imperial box at the Hippodrome, flank
the courtyard of the mosque. To the right
of the main building of the mosque are
the mausoleums of Süleyman and his
principal wife Haseki Hürrem, who is
known in the literature of Western Europe by the name Roxelane.

The side of the mosque facing away
from the Golden Horn preserves other
buildings from the complex, including
the kitchen for the poor, a school and
a caravanserai. Don't fail to stop at the
pleasant neighbouring tea garden *(daily
10am–6pm). Tiryaki Çarşısı Sok. | Mimar
Sinan Cad. | Süleymaniye*

These massive city walls have defied the passage of time for centuries

⑪ AQUEDUCT OF VALENS (BOZDOĞAN KEMERI)
(128 A2–3) (⫪ F5)

This 800-metre-long aqueduct is one of the most striking monuments remaining from the early Byzantine period. It was built in the second half of the 4th century under Emperor Valens to provide water for the city. Along with the Yerebatan Cistern, the Aqueduct of Valens is the most impressive reminder of the engineering skills of the Roman Empire. *On Atatürk Bulvarı | Aksaray*

⑫ YEDIKULE (130 C5) (⫪ 0)

Yedikule ('Seven Towers') is a fortress at the exact intersection of the Theodosian city wall on the landward side with the wall bordering the Sea of Marmara. It is a mixture of Byzantine and Ottoman elements. Within the walls of the fort you'll see the *Golden Gate*, through which Byzantine emperors rode in triumphal parades after victory in battle. In the Ottoman era the fortress was a dungeon for prominent prisoners. Today INSIDER TIP concerts are held here in summer. *Tue–Sun 9am–5pm | admission approx. £ 2.50 | Yedikule Meydanı*

BEYOĞLU

Pera, the old European quarter of İstanbul, is called Beyoğlu today. In the Byzantine age it was home to the Genoese, Venetians, French and other Europeans who traded with the orient.

Taksim Square is the central point of this district, where almost all diplomatic representations can be found. From the financial district of Karaköy on the Golden Horn and the Galata Tower, the avenue İstiklal Caddesi leads to the hub of İstanbul's traffic at Taksim Square. All the fascinating contrasts of this city meet here, from mystic dervishes to Christian Dior. After a period of decay, this quarter has now become *the* up-and-coming part of the city. This is the place to catch the rhythm of contemporary İstanbul, as Beyoğlu is the heart of the city's nightlife, where all the good bars, clubs and traditional taverns *(meyhane)* are to be found. People who rave about the cool scene in İstanbul are referring to Beyoğlu and the area around Taksim Square. Culturally, too, this is an interesting district: theatres, the opera, cinemas, jazz clubs, bookshops and attractive cafés pull in the public round the clock.

1 DOLMABAHÇE PALACE (DOLMA-BAHÇE SARAYI) (125 F1) *(Ⓜ L–M1)*

This palace on the Bosphorus covering an area of 250,000 m² was built in 1856 and soon became the new residence of the sultans. As western influences on the Ottoman Empire increased, Sultan Abdülmecit left the Topkapı Palace and moved here. Gold, marble and crystal were lavishly used to adorn the palace, and the furniture came from Paris and Prague. The enormous residence with its 500-m waterfront façade bears the hall-marks of the Balyan family, Armenian architects, four generations of whom embellished İstanbul with showy Neoclassical buildings. Dolmabahçe Palace now houses the deathbed of Mustafa Kemal Atatürk, the founder of the modern Turkish republic. It is guarded by soldiers round the clock.

The palace was comprehensively renovated in the 1990s and is now open to visitors, who are obliged to join one of two guided tours: one of them leading through the public apartments, the other through the old harem and the sultan's private quarters. If you want to see all of it, be sure to arrive no later than 1pm. *Tue, Fri–Sun 9am–3pm | admission approx. £ 8 | Dolmabahçe Cad. | Dolmabahçe*

2 GALATA TOWER (GALATA KULESI) ★ ☆ (124 B4) *(Ⓜ H4)*

The Galata Tower was built in 1348 by Genoese colonists in Constantinople. It is situated in the district of Karaköy

The sultans' splendour: a tour of the Dolmabahçe Palace

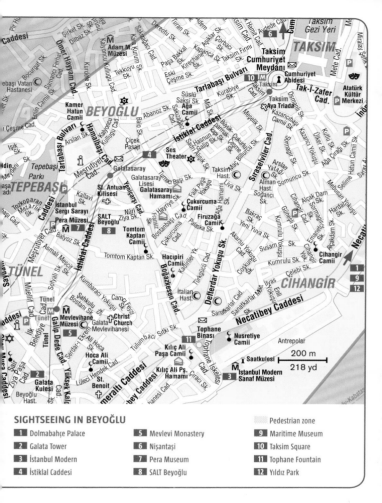

SIGHTSEEING IN BEYOĞLU

1 Dolmabahçe Palace
2 Galata Tower
3 İstanbul Modern
4 İstiklal Caddesi
5 Mevlevi Monastery
6 Nişantaşi
7 Pera Museum
8 SALT Beyoğlu
9 Maritime Museum
10 Taksim Square
11 Tophane Fountain
12 Yıldız Park

Pedestrian zone

and at the time of its construction was the tallest part of fortifications that surrounded the whole settlement. The tower rises 203 ft above the Golden Horn and has an open gallery below the top of the tower, from which a wonderful panorama of what was once the European quarter takes in the famous view of Sultanahmet and Beyazıt – a popular spot for filmmakers! You can take a lift up the tower, then pass a restaurant to the steps leading up to the viewing gallery. *Daily 8.30am–8pm for visitors | admission approx. £ 3.50 | Hendek Cad. | www.galatatower.net*

Mecca for Turkish and international contemporary art: İstanbul Modern

▪3 İSTANBUL MODERN (MODERN SANAT MÜZESI) ★ ●
(124 C4) (*∅ J4*)

A remarkable external appearance is matched by attractive contents: İstanbul's first private museum for contemporary Turkish art has found a home in warehouse no. 4 of the old harbour in Karaköy. It has 8000 m2 of exhibition space for outstanding works by modern Turkish artists, from painting and photography to video installations, from the 19th century to the present day. The rooms of the museum are laid out in a clear and simple design. Many in the art scene see the İstanbul Modern, which is supported by a private foundation, as taking up the banner of the MoMA and other major galleries – an ambition underpinned by changing exhibitions of international standing. A bookshop and a INSIDERTIP café on the waterfront with a view of the Topkapı Palace add to the attractions. *Tue–Sun 10am–6pm, Thu 10am–8pm | admission approx. £ 2.50 (Thu 10am–2pm free admission) | Meclis-i Mebusan Cad. | Liman Sahasi, Antrepo no. 4 | Karaköy | www.istanbulmodern.org*

▪4 İSTIKLAL CADDESI ★ ●
(124–125 B–D 2–4) (*∅ H–J 2–3*)

The pedestrian zone with its old-fashioned tram forms the lively heart of European İstanbul. This historic boulevard runs through Beyoğlu, an area that is a synonym for westernisation, from the upper exit of the Tünel funicular to Taksim Square. If you want to spend time at the cinema, a bar, a café or a music club in İstanbul, this is where you will surely end up. However, it is not just an entertainment strip: numerous bookshops, including second-hand bookshops, and galleries make the street a cultural attraction, and there are churches to visit too. Along the lower section foreign consulates lie hidden behind high walls, many of them sumptuous buildings that have survived from the Ottoman period, when they were embassies. Other buildings such as the Galatasaray Lycée and big arcades of shops serve as a reminder that in the late

19th century many rich Europeans lived here. One thing to bear in mind: on Saturday nights and Sundays the street is extremely crowded! *Take the trip up from Karaköy on the Tünel or walk from Taksim Square*

5 MEVLEVI MONASTERY (GALATA MEVLEVIHANESI) (124 B4) (*H3*)

Founded in 1491 the old Dervish monastery of Galata, the first Sufi monastery in İstanbul, still regularly stages INSIDERTIP performances of the Whirling Dervishes *(sema)* in a historic setting. On 17 December, to commemorate the death of Rumi (called Mevlana in Turkish), the founder of the sect, a special ceremony is held. Furthermore the Mevlevi Monastery is a *Sufi Museum* and a museum of divan literature. Precious manuscripts by Ottoman poets are on display. *Oct–April daily 3 and 4.30pm, May–Sept 5 and 6pm | admission approx. £ 2.50 | Galip Dede Cad. 15 | Tünel | tel. 0535 2 10 45 65 | www.mekder.org*

6 NİŞANTAŞI (131 D4) (*O*)

To the north of Taksim Square lie the middle-class residential and commercial districts of İstanbul. Nişantaşı has many boutiques, cafés and art galleries. There is a whiff of Paris in the air, ladies here are dressed en vogue when they take their dogs for a walk. In the alleys around the intersection shops are lined up one next to the other. If you get caught up in this style of city life, a good place to round off a shopping trip is the high-class *Kanyon* arcade (see chapter on Shopping) in Levent.

7 PERA MUSEUM (124 B3) (*H3*)

The Pera Museum, which opened in 2005, is a must for all lovers of art. Suna and İnan Kiraç, patrons of the arts, bought a house dating from 1893 in Tepebaşı and turned it into a fashionable urban museum. Permanent exhibitions such as the couple's collection of calligraphy fill the rooms. *Tue–Sat 10am–7pm, Sun midday–6pm | Meşrutiyet Cad. 141 | Tepebaşı | www.pm.org.tr*

8 INSIDERTIP SALT ●

Everyone who wants to get to know İstanbul's art scene should visit SALT. In 2011 the Şahenk family, owners of the Garanti Bank, gathered together all their art and cultural institutions, previously scattered in different locations, under one roof here – or to be

The heart of the city: İstiklal Caddesi boulevard

more exact under two roofs: the main building *(SALT Beyoğlu)* on İstiklal Caddesi was constructed between 1850 and 1860. The İstanbul star architect Han Tümertekin restored it. Its six floors are devoted to changing exhibitions of Turkish and European avant-garde art. The second building *(SALT Galata)* houses the museum of banking and archives of business and social affairs. Seminar rooms, a large library and studios are also on site. The building was originally designed by a French resident of the city, Alexandre Vallaury. In 1892 the Ottoman Empire's first central bank, *the Banque Impériale Ottomane (Bank-ı Osmanî-i Şahane)* opened here. *SALT Beyoğlu: Tue–Sat midday–8pm, Sun 10.30am–6pm | İstiklal Cad. 136* (124 B3) *(ⓜ H3); SALT Galata: Mon–Sat 10am–6pm | Bankalar (Voyvoda) Cad. 35–37* (124 B5) *(ⓜ H4) | free admission | www.saltonline.org*

▒9 MARITIME MUSEUM (DENIZ MÜZESI) (131 D4) *(ⓜ M1)*

This is not purely a naval museum, as it gives a good account of maritime activity in the Ottoman Empire as a whole. For those with nautical interests it is a little treasure trove, showing Ottoman sea charts and navigational instruments in addition to lots of model ships. A particularly impressive feature is the INSIDERTIP collection of historic sultans' barges. *Fri–Tue 9am–5pm | admission approx. £ 4 | Barbaros Hayrettin Paşa İskelesi Sok. | Beşiktaş*

▒10 TAKSIM SQUARE (TAKSIM MEYDANI) (125 D2) *(ⓜ K2)*

The Monument to the Republic *(Cumhuriyet Anıtı)* stands at the centre of the city's biggest square, which is also the one with the heaviest traffic. Taksim Square was laid out in the 1930s as a symbol of the modern republic. In the 1970s it became the most prominent place in İstanbul for demonstrations. One event that has not been forgotten is the demonstration of 1 May 1977: the participants met provocation from the ultra-right, and the event ended in bloodshed with many fatalities.

Thanks to the opera house, hotels and banks, Taksim is today a peaceful advertisement for a prosperous new İstanbul. The literal translation of its name is 'distributor' – in the Ottoman period there was a central water reservoir here. Now buses and the Metro depart from Taksim to all corners of the city. Around Taksim Square you will also find the stopping

KEEP FIT!

Jogging in İstanbul? At first sight this is hard to imagine. This enormous city is clogged up with traffic, and it is by no means easy to find a good circuit. However, dedicated joggers have a few options for working off energy: the best routes for runners are on the European shore of the Bosphorus (between Arnavutköy and Bebek) and on the Asian side on the Sea of Marmara (between Fenerbahçe and Bostancı).

In Yıldız Park and Emirgan Park too you can have a really good run. If you prefer other sporting activities, use a gym and indoor pool in one of the big hotels. There are hardly any public swimming baths in İstanbul.

The historic tram starts and turns round on Taksim Square

places of pool taxis, known as *dolmuş*, which are the fastest and cheapest way of getting to the outlying suburbs. *Taksim*

11 TOPHANE FOUNTAIN (TOPHANE ÇEŞMESI) (124 C4) (∅ J3)

In Tophane, at the end of the harbour area of Karaköy, there is a very fine example of an Ottoman fountain. Restored in 2001, the marble reliefs of the fountain, which was constructed in 1732 in the European Baroque style, are today a resplendent, immaculate white once again.

On the opposite side of the road is *Tophane*, the cannon foundry that Sultan Mehmet II established in 1453 shortly after the conquest of Constantinople. The massive building is no longer used for casting cannons, but has been restored and is an exhibition space for artists.

12 YILDIZ PARK (YILDIZ SARAYI/ YILDIZ PARKI) (131 D4) (∅ 0)

Sultan Abdulhamid II (1876–1909) lived and worked for decades behind the high walls of the Yıldız Palace, which was built for him on the slopes of Beşiktaş on the Bosphorus. The walls enclose a city within the city, an enormous complex which included the sultan's palace, the harem, small chalets, ornamental ponds, greenhouses and accommodation for the staff. From a pharmacy to a zoo, here the sultan had everything that his family needed to carry on their lives. Today ● *Yıldız Park* provides a green lung for the city. The largest pavilion (*Malta Köşkü*) was once used for state receptions and now harbours a museum. *Malta Köşkü* and the *Çadır Pavilion* are also open to visitors, who find cafés there (*daily 10am–6pm*). You can take a walk here in peace, especially on weekdays, and imagine how the sultans once took pleasure in the park. *Oct–May daily 9am–6pm, June–Sept daily 9am–8pm | entrance from Çırağan Cad. | Beşiktaş*

The former *hunting lodge* above Yıldız Parks is a little gem. It was built in the early 19th century before the neo-Baroque phase and is now home to two museums and an institute for Islamic studies. Unfortunately access to the hunting lodge from the park is no longer permitted, so visitors enter not from the Bosphorus but via Barbaros Bulvarı. *Wed–Mon 10am–4pm | admission approx. £ 1 | Barbaros Bulvarı | Yıldız Cad., past the university | Beşiktaş*

ÜSKÜDAR

The Asian side of İstanbul was already a bridgehead to the Bosphorus in antiquity. From the 8th century Muslims and Crusaders pitched their tents here when laying siege to İstanbul.

In 1352, almost a century before they conquered Constantinople, the Ottoman Turks took possession of Üsküdar. When the conquest was complete, this became the largest Muslim quarter of İstanbul, and the traditional religious character of the district has remained to this day. Take a ferry or a motorboat from Eminönü, Karaköy, Kabataş or Beşiktaş across to the other side, and stroll through the narrow streets there. Many of the old wooden houses have been replaced by ugly *apartman* blocks, but in between them in many places you will find a mosque, the tomb of a holy man or the house of a sect. At the Leander Tower in Salacak there is a ❄ tea garden with a view across the water to the Topkapı Palace. Above Üsküdar in the direction of Kadıköy lies the biggest cemetery in İstanbul, Karacaahmet.

◼ ÇAMLICA HILL ❄ (131 D5) (ᗰ 0)

At 860 ft this hill above Üsküdar is the highest point in İstanbul. In spite of the TV masts that cover its summit, it is well worth going up the hill, as from a café you get a fantastic view over the Bosphorus and almost the entire city, even as far as the Black Sea in the north. *By taxi from the ferry quays in Üsküdar or in Kadıköy, approx. £ 4*

◼ INSIDER TIP FETHI PASHA PARK (FETHI PAŞA KORUSU) ❄ (131 D4) (ᗰ 0)

The park can be reached on foot from Üsküdar. It starts opposite the Dolmabahçe Palace and extends over the hills almost as far as the first Bosphorus bridge. From a café and restaurant at a higher elevation you have a panoramic view of İstanbul. The mixed broadleaf and coniferous woods look lovely in autumn, and often have a covering of snow in winter. In spring rare Judas trees blossom here in various shades of purple. *Fethi Paşa Korusu | Paşalimani*

◼ HAYDARPASHA STATION (HAYDARPAŞA GARI) (131 D5) (ᗰ 0)

This was to have been the starting point for a major German-Turkish oriental project, the Berlin-Baghdad Railway, which was intended to extend German power down to the Persian Gulf and created tension with the British Empire. The splendid station was built on the Asian shore of the Bosphorus, directly opposite the Topkapı Palace. The first steam locomotive left in 1873. The station as it is today was completed by German architects in 1908. The Berlin-Baghdad Railway never reached its designated terminus far away to the southeast, however.

There are plans to close Haydarpasha down – the trains would then depart from the newly built stations of the Bosphorus Tunnel. Citizens of İstanbul are campaigning vigorously against plans of the city government to convert the station into a luxury hotel. They propose that it should be a municipal museum. *İstasyon Cad. | Haydarpaşa*

4 INSIDER TIP ▸ KUZGUNCUK
(131 D4) (*𝑀 0*)

This picturesque quarter, a popular set for the Turkish film industry, is one of

– signs of a multicultural life that has admittedly declined somewhat due to the exodus of Jews to Israel and the arrival of fishermen from regions on the Black Sea, but is still intact. *Ferry/Bus from Beşiktaş, taxi/on foot from Üsküdar*

5 LEANDER TOWER (131 D5) (*𝑀 0*)

The 'Maiden's Tower' was built in the 18th century on a tiny island near the Asian shore and close to the entrance to the Bosphorus. During the day it serves

The Asian part of İstanbul begins here: view from the ferry to Üsküdar

the few villages on the Bosphorus that have retained their old character. Situated between the centre of Üsküdar and the first Bosphorus bridge, Kuzguncuk is a place of wooden houses and villas that have been lovingly restored by artists and intellectuals.

Once a Jewish settlement, Kuzguncuk still has one of the most frequented synagogues of the city, next to which a church and a mosque can be found too

as a café, and in the evening becomes a fashionable restaurant with live music. Beware: this is an expensive hangout! According to legend the Leander Tower was built as a safe place for a sultan's daughter. A fortune-teller had prophesied that she would fall victim to a snakebite. Another tale from Greek mythology relates that Leander swam every evening across the Hellespont to come to his lover Hero in the tower. He

İSTANBUL BOĞAZI

Üsküdar Vapur İskelesi
III. Ahmet Çeş.

Eminönü

Kabataş

Üsküdar Feribot
İskelesi

Semsi Ahmet Paşa
Camii

Kız Kulesi

SIGHTSEEING IN ÜSKÜDAR

- **1** Çamlıca Hill
- **2** Fethi Pasha Park
- **3** Haydarpasha Station
- **4** Kuzguncuk
- **5** Leander Tower
- **6** Mihrimah Sultan Mosque
- **7** Şemsi Pasha Mosque

finally drowned while making the crossing, at which the grieving Hero hurled herself into the sea from the top of the tower. *Tue–Sun 10am–11pm | tel. 0216 3 42 47 47 | www.kizkulesi.com.tr | crossing from Üsküdar, directly opposite the tower, or from Ortaköy and Sarayburnuon on the European side for approx. £ 3.50 (incl. one drink), in the evening only from Üsküdar and Ortaköy*

6 MIHRIMAH SULTAN MOSQUE (MIHRIMAH SULTAN CAMII)
(131 D5) (*ℳ 0*)

The complex of buildings opposite the ferry quays of Üsküdar is one of the masterpieces of the great palace architect Sinan. It was commissioned by Mihrimah Sultan, a daughter of Suleiman the Magnificent, and completed in 1548. Here Sinan took inspiration from

Setting for a tragic love story: the Leander Tower

the ground plan of Hagia Sophia, with the exception that there is no semi-dome over the entrance area. After entering the mosque you are immediately standing beneath the main dome. *Daily except when prayers are being held | Üsküdar Meydanı*

▣ ŞEMSI PASHA MOSQUE (ŞEMSI PAŞA CAMII) (131 D5) *(Ⓜ 0)*

Right on the shore in Üsküdar opposite the Topkapı Palace stands one of the most beautiful mosques in the whole of İstanbul. It was built in 1580 by the great Sinan and is close to the Leander Tower, making it easy to combine visits to these two sights.

MORE SIGHTS

Many visitors to İstanbul get no further than the historic city centre and the İstiklal Caddesi boulevard in Beyoğlu – which means they miss out on some of the most beautiful sights in the city.
İstanbul is a fathomless well of interesting experiences, which shows visitors its most likeable side when seen from the sea. These places round about the Bosphorus can conveniently be reached by ferry, bus, dolmuş or taxi.

ARNAVUTKÖY ☼
(131 D4) *(Ⓜ 0)*

The name Arnavutköy means 'village of the Albanians', a reference to the fact that this place was built by Albanian immigrants in the 15th century. Later many İstanbul Greeks lived here. Like many other settlement on the Bosphorus, Arnavutköy stretches along a dried-up tributary of the straits. By the sea there are some highly recommendable

Relax on the Bosphorus: street cafés by the quay in Beylerbeyi

fish restaurants, e.g. INSIDERTIP *Adem Baba (daily | Satışmeydanı Sok. 2 | www.adembaba.com | Budget)*. The hill behind Arnavutköy holds the campus of the renowned Boğaziçi University, and further north you are approaching the *Akıntı burnu*: 'Cape Current', where at the surface the waters of the Black Sea flow at a speed of no less than twelve miles per hour – which means this is definitely not a place for swimming! *Bus and dolmuş from Beşiktaş*

BEYLERBEYI PALACE (BEYLERBEYI SARAYI) (131 E3) (*ฌ 0*)

The palace, one of the most important in İstanbul, lies at the foot of the first Bosphorus bridge on the Asian side. It was built between 1861 and 1865 for Sultan Abdülaziz. For a long time the palace served as a summer residence for the sultan and his family. Previously a 16th-century wooden palace occupied the site. The architect took as his model the typical Ottoman house and grouped the rooms of each wing around a central courtyard *(sofa)*. The sumptuous furnishings of the men's wing have been preserved. The two kiosks in the garden and the stables should also not be missed.

After visiting the palace it's a good idea to eat lunch by the boat quays of Beylerbeyi nearby. On the banks of the Bosphorus in Beylerbeyi there is also an attractive ● *promenade* where you can stretch your legs beneath the plane trees. *Tue, Wed, Fri–Sun 9.30am–5pm, Oct–Feb until 4pm | Beylerbeyi Sarayı | Çayırbaşı Durağı | Beylerbeyi-Üsküdar | tel. 0216 3219320*

BOAT TRIP ON THE BOSPHORUS ★ ●

The long boat tour on the Bosphorus is one of the very best activities that İstanbul can offer. On the way you pass modern architecture and historic sights, high-class residential areas and charming fishing villages – and you see the green slopes on the shore in all their glory. The trip on the municipal ferry starts in Eminönü and goes out almost as far as the Black Sea. It finishes in the village Anadolu Kavağı to the northeast, where lunch in one of the fish restaurants can be recommended. Before boarding the ferry back to the city centre, you can walk up the hill to the ruin of a Byzantine castle, which affords a superb view of the mouth of the Bosphorus. The trip to Anadolu Kavağı takes 125 minutes, and you should plan a whole day for the return journey with a lunch break. *Fare (return) approx. £ 8 | departure from Boğaz Hattı quay in Eminönü (127 D2) (∅ H5) June–Sept daily 10.35am, noon and 1.30pm | return from Anadolu Kavağı daily 3 and 4.15pm, Mon–Fri also 5pm, Sat–Sun also 6pm*

`INSIDER TIP` **EMIRGAN PARK (EMIRGAN PARKI) ●** 🌿 **(131 D3) (∅ O)**
This wonderful park above the Bosphorus village of Emirgan is famous for its show

of tulips and its three little pavilions. When the tulip festival is held in April, the park is a sea of colour in countless shades. By the way: tulips came from Turkey to Holland and not vice versa, as many people believe today. The three pavilions in the park are called, according to their colours, the White, the Yellow and the Pink Pavilion. They date from the 19th century and are open to the public with their terraces in use as cafés or teahouses. From the Pink Pavilion there is a fantastic view of the Bosphorus. Down by the sea, tea is served from a samovar. *Closed in winter | entrance from Emirgan | bus or taxi from Beşiktaş*

ORTAKÖY (131 D4) (∅ O)
Ortaköy is the first former fishing village on the Bosphorus that you encounter going out from Taksim. From the shore it spreads up the hill above the strait. This has always been a place where different cultures met: two churches, a synagogue and a mosque lie close together near the water. ● *Ortaköy Square* is a pleasant spot to take a break: take in the view of the Bosphorus or watch what's going

RELAX & CHILL OUT

Time spent in a Turkish bath is not just a matter of bodily cleanliness. A massage, a cold drink in the cooling-down area and the friendly service are also healing for the soul. Afterwards you feel as if you've been born again. In the hamam you get everything that you need for taking a bath, but of course you can also bring your own things with you. Women cover their upper body with a bath towel, while men wrap it round their hips. It is not the done thing to

appear completely naked in the presence of the staff. In the ● *Galatasaray Hamami* in Beyoğlu, which is more than 500 years old, mystic flute sounds fill the domed space. *Daily 8am–8pm for women, until 10pm for men, June–Sept one hour longer | admission £ 18, with peeling £ 25, cellulite and aromatherapy massage extra | Turnacibasi Sok. 24 (124 C3) (∅ J2) | Galatasaray | tel. 0212 2 49 43 42*

Low horsepower: traffic on the Princes' Island of Büyükada

on in the village. In the 1980s young artists discovered the charm of Ortaköy and opened studios and bookshops here. The old buildings were restored and turned into cafés and restaurants. At the weekends there is a buzzing, flourishing art market in the quarter. The landmark of this place is the delicate-looking Baroque *Ortaköy Mosque* with its two slender minarets. In the 19th century the sultan used to come across from the Dolmabahçe Palace in his stately barge to take part in Friday prayers. *Bus from Beşiktaş*

PRINCES' ISLANDS (ADALAR) ⭐
(0) (𝄚 0)

Once a place of exile for Byzantine princes, today the islands to the southeast of İstanbul are a delightful destination for excursions for locals and tourists. In summer countless visitors to the islands flock to the shores where bathing is possible. No motorised traffic is allowed on the islands. Alongside bicycles *(rental from £ 2.50)* horse-drawn carriages are the sole means of transport available. Of the five inhabited islands ● *Büyükada* is the largest and gets the most visitors. A complete circuit of the island in a horse-drawn carriage *(fayton)* costs approx. £ 25 and lasts one hour, including a tea break. The nearest island to Büyükada is *Kınalıadad*, where most of the residents are İstanbul Armenians. *Burgazada* is the one where the city's wealthiest people have their summer retreats. A pretty fishing harbour with taverns and the little bay of Kalpazankaya on the south side of the island where swimming is possible have made it popular with İstanbul's bohemian scene. The next port of call for ferries and speedboats is *Heybeliada*, where the Turkish navy maintains a training base. Middle-class İstanbul people live here all year round and give the island the character of a metropolitan suburb. The smallest inhabited island, *Sedef*, is beyond Büyükada. Not many make the trip out there, as it is privately owned by a family. A handful of people own summer villas there and do not welcome strangers who come to walk around or swim. *City ferries (Ada Vapuru) from Kabataş and Bostancı (to get to Bostancı take a dolmuş from Taksim Square) | timetables at www.sehirhatlari.com.tr; fast 'sea buses' (Deniz Otobüsü) from Kabataş | www.ido.com.tr; motor boats operated by the private Mavi Marmara company from Bostancı and Kabataş | www.mavimarmara.net; tickets cost between £ 1 and £ 3 | length of journey, depending on starting point and destination, between 30 and 90 min.*

RUMELI FORTRESS (RUMELI HISARI)
(131 D4) *(𝄐 0)*

Sultan Mehmet II, who later conquered Constantinople for the Ottoman Turks, is said to have drawn up the plan of the fortress with his own hand, which is why when seen from above it spells out the word 'Mehmet' in Arabic letters. This is the story told by one of İstanbul's numerous legends. It is certainly the case that the fortress, which was completed in 1452, played a major role in the taking of Constantinople by the Turks. At the narrowest point on the Bosphorus it lies directly opposite its counterpart on the Asian side, Anadolu Hisari, and so ensured effective control of the straits. On display In the grounds of the fortress is part of the chain that the Turks used to close the Bosphorus to ships that tried to come to the aid of the Byzantine defenders of the city during the siege of Constantinople. In summer concerts are held in the castle theatre. *Thu–Tue 9.30am–4.30pm | Yahya Kemal Cad. 42 | Sariyer | tel. 0212 2 63 53 05*

SABANCI MUSEUM (SSM)
(131 D3) *(𝄐 0)*

The Sabancı dynasty is one of the richest Turkish families of industrialists. Their interests are not confined to making money, as this museum shows. They have converted their wonderful urban villa into a private museum. In addition to permanent exhibitions of works by Ottoman Turkish painters, spectacular temporary exhibitions are held several times a year – e.g. of works by Picasso and Rodin. *Tue, Thu–Sun 10am–6pm, Wed 10am–8pm | admission £ 2 | Atlı Köşk Emirgan | muze.sabanciuniv.edu*

The Rumeli Fort testifies to the Ottoman siege

FOOD & DRINK

In İstanbul satisfying your hunger is no more than a pleasant side-effect of eating: here people sit down at home around the table in order to be with their families, and go out to a restaurant in order to chat with friends and celebrate.

Since the Byzantine period the cuisine of İstanbul has been a synthesis of butter, olive oil, pasta, fish, meat and dairy dishes. Today, sushi and pizza are also available. Fish of course takes pride of place on the menu. Many kinds of fish are tastiest when grilled, e.g. *lüfer* (bluefish), *palamut* (bonito) and *sardalya* (sardines); other kinds are best fried: *kalkan* (turbot), *barbunya* (red mullet) and *hamsi* (Black Sea sardines). It's also worth trying sea bass *(levrek)* or prawns

baked with mushrooms, tomatoes and melted cheese *(karides güveç)*. Kılıç (swordfish) on a skewer is a real delicacy. Squid *(ahtapot)* is eaten as a salad and king prawns *(böcek)* are grilled. Don't be shy about asking the price – fish is often priced by weight.

To start the day, people in İstanbul are content to eat some white bread with olives, sheep's cheese and honey, washed down with tea. Most hotels provide an opulent breakfast buffet. Lunch is generally not a heavy meal in İstanbul. The best thing to do is to go to one of the little places *(lokanta)* where the locals eat in their own neighbourhood. Here you will get good, down-to-earth food: a tomato *(domates)* or lentil soup *(mercimek çorbası)*; meatballs *(köfte)*, chicken with

Photo: Pandeli Restaurant in Eminönü

Ancient Byzantine coins bore the sign of fish from the Bosphorus – today it comes to the table fresh from the sea

rice *(tavuklu pilav)*, the famous *döner kebap* or a seasonal vegetable dish *(sebze)*. Note that most eateries outside the city centre serve no alcohol. Otherwise the evening meal is marked by certain rituals for the inhabitants of the city: first of all drinks are served – either rakı, a strong aniseed-based spirit, beer *(bira)* or wine *(şarap)*. Where beer is concerned, *Efes* pils is a good choice, and among the wines you might want to sample a dry white such as *Çankaya, Sarafin, Sevilen* or *Kavaklıdere Narince,* or if you prefer red

perhaps *Corvus, Signium* or *Antik,* also called *Angora.* Make a selection of a few pre-prepared starters *(meze)* and wait for the warm intermediate course that you have ordered. After a while, and this can easily mean an hour, you order your main dish: either fish or meat. When it comes to desserts, Arabian and Persian influences are in evidence. Examples of this are *baklava,* thin flaky pastry filled with pistachios or walnuts and steeped in syrup, and various milk-based puddings *(muhallebi).* Turkish people like

Dine in pleasant surroundings on the roof – in Fransiz Sokaği

to eat fresh fruit *(meyve)* for dessert. To round things off you drink mocha: *sade* (without sugar), *orta* (medium sweet) or *şekerli* (sweet), and nowadays sometimes with added mastic resin *(sakızlı)*.

CAFÉS & SNACK BARS

CAFÉ MAGNAURA ⋇ (129 E6) *(ⓜ J8)*
This café has tables on two floors and an attractive viewing terrace. Come here for breakfast or lunch, or for light meals in the evening (steaks, shrimps or chicken). *Daily 9am–1am | Akbıyık Cad. 27 | Sultanahmet | tel. 0212 5 18 76 22*

ÇORLULU ALİ PAŞA MEDRESESİ ● (128 C4) *(ⓜ G7)*
In the early 18th century the treasurer of the Ottoman court, Çorlulu Ali Paşa, built

a college. Its courtyard is today home to a shady tea garden with a mystic atmosphere. It is a popular haunt of all sections of the population, including groups of women, and is famous for its hookah pipes. Mocha brewed over charcoal goes well with a leisurely smoke. *Daily 7am–2am | Yeniçeriler Cad. 34 | Beyazıt*

INSIDER TIP ▶ ÇUKURKEYİF BAHÇE (124 C3) *(ⓜ J3)*
This little gem is hidden away in the antiques quarter of Çukurcuma below İstiklal Caddesi: relax in a vine-covered garden, away from the bustle of the city. Snacks, home-made pasta, light dishes with chicken. *Daily 10am–2am | Altıpatlar Çık. 4 | Galatasaray-Çukurcuma | Beyoğlu | tel. 0212 2 51 11 93*

FRENCH STREET (FRANSIZ SOKAĞI) (124 C3) *(ⓜ J2–3)*
This is nowadays the name for what was once called Cezayir Sokak (Algeria Street). Buildings renovated with the help of the Institut Français are now home to countless galleries, cafés and restaurants. Two of the best are *Les Zazoues* and *Desire* (both daily). *Galatasaray | Fransız Sok. | Beyoğlu*

INSIDER TIP GEZİ (125 D2) *(ⓜ K2)*
Although it is located on Taksim Square, this patisserie is still an oasis. In summer you can sit in the small front garden. It's not a cheap café, but the biscuits and cakes are up there with the very best in the city. *Mon–Sat 7am–1am, Sun 8am–midnight | İnönü Cad. 5 | Taksim | tel. 0212 2 92 53 53 | www.geziistanbul.com*

LAVANTA ⏲ (131 D4) *(ⓜ 0)*
The İstanbul branch of a well-known café in Alaçatı near İzmir, where not only the furnishings come from the Aegean. All sorts of delicious salads and

light meals seasoned with olive oil are on the menu. You can also order an Aegean breakfast with fresh tomatoes and good cheese. The owner uses organically produced ingredients. *Daily 8am–2am | Mecidiye Köprü Sok. 16 | Ortaköy | tel. 0212 2272995 | www.lavantarestaurant.com*

LIMONLU BAHÇE ● (124 C3) (*ω J2*)

The 'lemon garden' at the heart of Pera, the old European quarter, is an ideal place to spend a few quiet hours in leafy surroundings. Guests can relax in hammocks. The house is famous for its soft drinks flavoured with mint and watermelon, as well as its own home-made liqueurs. *Daily 10am–midnight | Yeniçarşı Cad. 98 | Galatasaray*

LUCCA (131 D4) (*ω 0*)

This café in Bebek with a post-modern look is a good place to hang out at any time – for breakfast, cake and coffee in the afternoon or to spend a quiet moment with a glass of good wine. *Daily 10am–2am | Cevdetpaşa Cad. 51 B | Bebek*

MASAL EVİ (131 D5) (*ω 0*)

The cosy 'house of fairytales' occupies an old Ottoman building with a garden, where blues and jazz are played in relaxed surroundings. In the evening the music gets louder, and the three storeys morph into a bar. *Daily 10am–2am | Kadife Sok. 33 | Kadıköy | tel. 0216 4182753*

PİYER LOTİ (130 C4) (*ω 0*)

One of the city's most famous cafés, which now bears the name of Turkophile French novelist Pierre Loti (1850–1923), has looked down on the Golden Horn in Eyüp for 200 years. In winter it's cosy inside, in summer you can sit in the lovely garden. No alcohol! *Daily 8am–mid-night | Gümüşsuyu Cad., Balmumcu Sok. 5 | Eyüp | tel. 0212 5812696*

SAFİYE SULTAN (123 D1) (*ω E1*)

The industrial plants in Hasköy on the Golden Horn are being dismantled and a new urban area is taking shape. This Ottoman-style café with hookahs is housed in the 450-year-old former Eshger Synagogue. *Daily 9am–1am | Hasköy Cad. 1 | Haliç | tel. 0212 3614888*

MARCO POLO HIGHLIGHTS

★ **Banyan**
This restaurant with a terrace serves Far Eastern food with one of the city's finest views thrown in → p. 64

★ **Vogue**
Enjoy grilled fish and a glass of good wine with a panoramic view of İstanbul → p. 64

★ **İskele**
The furnishings in this restaurant are basic, but the seafood is the very best → p. 65

★ **Pandeli**
A most welcome stop-over while strolling around the Egyptian Bazaar: food for gourmets in surroundings to match → p. 65

★ **Kanaat Lokantası**
Get to know the centuries-old tradition of Turkish cuisine here → p. 70

★ **Moda Çay Bahçesi**
Rub shoulders with the people of İstanbul on a sunny afternoon and take pleasure in a wide-ranging sea view → p. 71

RESTAURANTS: EXPENSIVE

360 İSTANBUL ☽
(124 C4) (*Ⅲ H2*)

From Topkapı Palace to the Golden Horn and St Anthony's Church: high above the roofs of the city this wonderful location gives you a breathtaking all-round view! The glass-walled restaurant is situated in an Art Nouveau building. Reservations essential. *Daily | İstiklal Cad. 311 (Misir Apt.) | Beyoğlu | tel. 0212 2 51 10 42 | www.360istanbul.com*

AL JAMAL (125 D–E1) (*Ⅲ K1*)

İstanbul is discovering the Maghreb: along with North African food, this restaurant with Moroccan decor also stages INSIDER TIP belly dancing. Set menu only – drinks are included. Smart dress obligatory! *Daily from 7.30pm | Sun–Thu £ 60, Fri, Sat £ 65 | Taşkışla Cad. 13 | Maçka-Taksim | tel. 0212 2 31 03 56*

BANYAN ★ ☽ (131 D4) (*Ⅲ 0*)

Top-class Far Eastern dining on a terrace by the Bosphorus, with a view of the first bridge and the Ortaköy Mosque. High-quality, fashionable and a coveted address: definitely book in advance! *Daily | Sun breakfast buffet from 10am | Muallim Naci Cad. Salhane Sok. 3 | Ortaköy-Beşiktaş | tel. 0212 2 59 90 60 | www.banyanrestaurant.com*

CHANGA (125 D2) (*Ⅲ 0*)

Chic restaurant serving excellent fusion cuisine. You can watch the chef through a glass floor. With *Müzedechanga (closed Mon | Sakip Sabancı Cad. 22 | Emirgan | (131 D3) (Ⅲ 0))* the owners have opened a second popular estab-

GOURMET RESTAURANTS

Mikla ☽ (124 B3) (*Ⅲ H3*)

A gourmet restaurant on the top floor of the new Marmara-Pera Hotel. The 12-course 'tasting menu' runs from caviar to fillet steak and Turkish fusion cuisine for a price of around £ 50. The clientele, well-heeled but not chic, enjoy a breathtaking view. *Daily | The Marmara Pera | Meşrutiyet Cad. 1 | Beyoğlu-Taksim | tel. 0212 2 93 56 56 | www.istanbulyi.com*

Poseidon ☽ (131 D4) (*Ⅲ 0*)

Superb fish restaurant on the Bosphorus: fresh seafood, lovingly prepared and served on a waterfront terrace. *Menu approx. £ 50 | daily | Cevdet Paşa Cad. 58 | Bebek | tel. 0212 2 87 95 31 | www.poseidonbebek.com*

Tuğra ☽ (131 D4) (*Ⅲ 0*)

Savour refined Ottoman cuisine cooked to original recipes in the Çırağan Palace Hotel Kempinski with a great view of the Bosphorus. *Menu about £ 60 | Thu–Sun 7–11pm | Çırağan Cad. 32 | Beşiktaş | tel. 0212 3 26 46 46 | www.kempinski-istanbul.com*

Vogue ★ ☽ (131 D4) (*Ⅲ 0*)

Gourmet restaurant with diverse dishes: Mediterranean and fusion food on a lovely roof terrace, and a high-class sushi menu. Chef Ünal Yıldız recommends veal medallions and grilled halibut. *Menu about £ 60 | daily, sushi Mon–Sat | BJK Plaza | Spor Cad. 48 | Akaretler (Beşiktaş) | tel. 0212 2 27 44 04 | www.istanbuldoors.com*

The clue is in the name: 360 İstanbul enjoys a fantastic, all-round view

lishment INSIDER TIP on the roof of the Sabancı Museum. *Evenings only, closed Sun | Siraselviler Cad. 47 | Taksim | tel. 0212 2 51 70 64 | www.changa-istanbul. com*

İSKELE ⭐ (131 D4) (*Ø 0*)
One of the best fish restaurants in the city! On the disused ferry quay at Rumelihisari a great variety of seafood is served in plain surroundings. Chef Nuri Soysal recommends pike-perch from the oven. *Daily midday–midnight | Yahya Kemal Cad. 1 | Rumelihisari | tel. 0212 2 63 29 97 | www.rumelihisariiskele.com*

LİMAN LOKANTASI 🔅
(124 B5) (*Ø J4*)
This restaurant has been in business at the İstanbul harbour since 1951. Fine view of the Bosphorus, good Turkish-Ottoman dishes: kebabs, roast lamb and hot figs with ice cream to finish off. *Closed Tue | Rıhtım Cad. 52/3 | Karaköy | tel. 0212 2 92 39 93 | www.capacapa. com*

PANDELİ ⭐ (129 D2) (*Ø H5*)
Founded in 1956 by famous Greek chef Pandeli, this restaurant on the left above the entrance to the Spice Bazaar dishes up the best midday menu in the city, based on old Ottoman recipes. Queen Elizabeth and Mikhail Gorbachev were brought here to try it. *In summer daily 11.30am–7.30pm, in winter 11.30am–6.30pm | Mısır Çarşısı Eminönü | tel. 0212 5 27 39 09 | www.pandeli.com.tr*

PAPERMOON (131 D4) (*Ø 0*)
Really hip among İstanbul's smart set, with a lovely garden for dining in summer. The food is Italian and of extremely high quality. Its pasta creations are famous. No reservation? Forget it! *Daily midday–midnight | ground floor of the Akmerkez Residence | Nispetiye Cad. Etiler | tel. 0212 2 82 16 16 | www.papermoon. com.tr*

SARNIÇ LOKANTASI (129 E4) (*Ø J6*)
The candlelight dinner is an experience in this cistern converted to a high-class restaurant next to restored wooden

Çiçek Pasaji Art Nouveau arcade in Beyoğlu

calamari. A good address if you want to go on to the cinema, a concert or a bar afterwards. *Daily 7.30pm–4am, wine bar midday–2am | Sıraselviler | Çukurçeşme Sok. 13 | Taksim | tel. 0212 2 93 54 80 | www.zarifi.com.tr*

RESTAURANTS: MODERATE

INSIDER TIP ALEM (124 B–C2) (*∅ J2*)

The customers in this attractive rakı tavern are mainly locals. Listen to Turkish music, live and unplugged, and enjoy menus at under £ 16 as well as good starters. *Daily 11am–2am | Nevizade Sok. 4 C | Beyoğlu | tel. 0212 2 49 60 55*

AYAZPAŞA RUS LOKANTASI (125 E2) (*∅ K1*)

Founded in 1943 by Judith Krishanovski, a Hungarian Jew, and her Russian husband, this is one of İstanbul's long-established gourmet restaurants. Cemal Ok, who served for years as head waiter, took over in 1978 and continued to serve Russian food. His 'yellow vodka' *(sari vodka)* with lemon peel and cloves is famous all over the city. *Daily | İnönü Cad. 77/A | Gümüşsuyu | tel. 0212 2 43 48 92 | www.ayazpasaruslokantasi.com*

BALIKÇI SABAHATTIN (129 E5) (*∅ J7*)

'Fisherman Sabahattin' from Crete has been dishing up specialities such as rice with mussels in wine for 40 years. His various fish salads are also a delight for the palate. *Daily | Seyit Hasan Kuyu Sok. 1 | Cankurtaran | tel. 0212 4 58 18 24 | www.balikcisabahattin.com*

CARNE (131 D4) (*∅ 0*)

The only restaurant in the city that cooks strictly according to Jewish regulations. Kebabs made from kosher meat, pastry rolls with vegetables. *Mon–Thu midday–midnight, Fri midday–3pm, Sun midday–*

houses. Again: reservations are a muse! *Daily 7pm–midnight | Soğukçeşme Sok. (behind Hagia Sophia) | tel. 0212 5 12 42 91*

SPAZIO ☀ (125 D1) (*∅ K1*)

The Italian restaurant at the *Hyatt Regency* does excellent lamb and fish dishes as well as pizza and pasta, to be savoured while enjoying a view of the city and the garden. In the evening round off the meal at the hotel jazz club. *Mon–Sat 7pm–11pm | Hyatt Regency Hotel | Taşkışla Cad. Taksim | tel. 0212 2 25 70 00 | www. istanbul.grand.hyatt.com*

ZARIFI (124 C2) (*∅ J2*)

An old laundry turned into a restaurant is now a gourmet destination in Beyoğlu with typical local dishes such as stuffed

6pm | Muallim Naci Cad. 41 | Ortaköy | tel. 0212 2 60 84 25

ÇARŞI RAKI BALIK (131 D5) (*ฒ 0*)

At the market in Kadıköy on the Asian side there is a small but high-class alley with one seafood restaurant next to the other. Come for the fresh fish, or if you prefer vegetarian or meat dishes, and lots of delicious starters at a reasonable price. ● At weekends everybody watches football on the big screen next door! *Daily midday–midnight | Caferaga Mah. Günesli Bahce Sok. 37 | Kadıköy | tel. 0216 4 50 15 64*

ÇİÇEK PASAJI (124 C2) (*ฒ J2*)

Built in 1876 as a shopping arcade for florists, which is what the name means, this place is now filled with bars and restaurants. Recommended addresses here are *Ceneviz* (no. 12), *Huzur* (no. 18) and *Kimene* (no. 172/177). At weekends guests dance on the tables when the Romany music rouses them. Behind the arcade is Nevizade, a lane of taverns. *Daily | İstiklal Cad. | Galatasaray | Beyoğlu | www.tarihicicekpasaji.com*

DESPINA ⟡ (0) (*ฒ 0*)

Madame Despina's tavern in Tatavla, once largely a Greek quarter and now called Kurtuluş, has been going since 1946. Live Greek music and a set menu for approx. £ 16 are the attractions here – as well as a fine view of İstanbul. *Sun–Thu midday–midnight, Fri, Sat to 1am | Açıkyol Sok. 9 | Kurtuluş | Şişli | tel. 0212 2 47 33 57*

FAROS WINE & DINE (125 D2) (*ฒ K1*)

A high-quality eating scene has appeared around Taksim Square in the last couple of years, alongside the established array of taverns and night clubs. This restaurant has a good wine list, and the items on the menu are mainly Italian and international. Approx. £ 5 buys you a generous breakfast buffet till 11am, at the weekend until midday. *Daily 7.30am–1am | Cumhuriyet Cad. 34/A | Taksim | tel. 0212 2 97 60 77 | www.farostaksim.com*

INSIDER TIP ▶ HAZZO PULO
(124 B3) (*ฒ H2*)

Cosy wine bar on Galatasaray Square. Chef Feramuz Usta prepares cold and warm starters and dishes from the grill, but vegetarians need not go hungry either. Good-quality house wines are available at a fair price. Reservations are advised. *Daily midday–2am | Meşrutiyet Cad. 31 B | Beyoğlu/Galatasaray | tel. 0212 2 45 55 23*

İZ.NİK + ET ☺ (131 D4) (*ฒ 0*)

The proprietor comes from the green city of İznik, southeast of İstanbul. What sets this restaurant apart are the carefully selected ingredients: meat from free-range animals, organically produced olive oil and bread baked in a village to the west of İstanbul. A T-bone steak costs

LOW BUDGET

▶ Enjoy ice cream on the Bosphorus: at *Mini Dondurma* **(131 D4)** (*ฒ 0*) in Bebek, one of İstanbul's most beautiful bays, you get two scoops for less than £ 1. *Daily | Cevdet Paşa Cad. 107 | Bebek*

▶ Jam, cheese, sausage, eggs, olives and as much tea as you can drink: you can enjoy a cheap (£ 3.50) and excellent breakfast at *Özsüt* **(124 C2)** (*ฒ J2*). *Daily | İstiklal Cad. 206 | Taksim*

LOCAL SPECIALITIES

▶ **farjantin** – beer with a shot of vodka: cheap and not without after-effects!

▶ **arnavut ciğeri** – tender fried pieces of lamb's liver with onions

▶ **ayva tatlısı** – dessert consisting of half a quince, cooked with sugar and cinnamon, topped off with cream

▶ **baklava** – a fine dessert made of many layers of puff pastry filled with walnuts or pistachios. Very, very sweet! (photo left)

▶ **cacık** – yoghurt with garlic and bits of cucumber

▶ **çerkeztavuğu** – ‚Cherkessian chicken': chicken breast, walnuts, milk and flour, a real delicacy usually served cold

▶ **çiroz salatası** – salad of air-dried sprats or very small mackerel

▶ **iç pilav** – a rice dish with raisins, nuts and pieces of liver

▶ **imambayıldı** – ‚the imam fainted': a hors d'oeuvre made from aubergines with garlic

▶ **kadınbudu köfte** – ‚women's legs' made from minced meat, rice and egg yolk, fried in a pan

▶ **karides güveç** – shrimps, tomatoes and mushrooms covered in cheese and baked

▶ **kaymaklı kadayif** – a delicate dessert of pastry with cream

▶ **kefal pilakisi** – mullet, roasted in the oven in its own juice and served luke-warm with vegetables

▶ **külbastı** – tender slices of lamb fillet, seasoned with thyme and grilled without oil

▶ **lakerda** – a genuine İstanbul delight: tuna marinated in salt: don't miss it!

▶ **midye dolması** – mussels stuffed with raisin rice

▶ **paçanga böreği** – flaky pastry stuffed with air-dried ham

▶ **rakı** – this strong, clear aniseed spirit is drunk diluted with water, which makes it milky, or neat

▶ **sarı votka** – vodka, flavoured with lemon and matured for a long period

▶ **sigara böreği** – a roll of flaky pastry with sheep's cheese and parsley

▶ **topik** – Armenian starter made from puréed chickpeas

▶ **yeşil salata** – lettuce salad, often including finely chopped red cabbage and grated carrot

▶ **zeytinyağlı dolmalar** – stuffed paprika or vine leaves in oil, served cold as a starter (photo right)

around £ 12, a delicious dessert no more than £ 2.50. Lots of good, meat-free salads are also on offer. This is an ideal stopping-off point after a shopping tour north of Taksim Square. There is lots of space inside at the back or in the garden. *Mon–Sat 10am–11pm, Sun 11am–10pm | Teşvikiye Cad. 20 | Nişantaşı | tel. 0212 2 96 48 60 | www.izniket.com*

KHORASANI (129 E5) (*ID H7*)

The Turkish *Ocakbaşı* ('at the oven') style of eating gathers diners around an open grill where the meat is cooked, preferably on a skewer. The cooks prepare the dishes, and guests enjoy starters while waiting for their main course. This kebab house in the city centre also has a regular restaurant on the upper floor. *Daily midday–midnight, Fri, Sat (with live music) until 2am | Divanyolu Cad. Ticarethane Sok. 39–41 | Sultanahmet | tel. 0212 5 19 59 59 | www.khorasani restaurant.com*

KOÇO ☆ (131 D5) (*ID 0*)

This excellent and fashionable fish restaurant is situated on the Asian side of the city at the tip of the Moda peninsula, which translates into a wonderful view from the terrace to the marina of Fenerbahçe on the Sea of Marmara. *Daily | Moda Cad. 265 | Kadıköy | tel. 0216 3 36 07 95*

ÖRDEKLI BAKKAL SOKAK (128 B5–6) (*ID G7–8*)

This place is not merely a single good fish restaurant, but several of them. On the Sea of Marmara, Greeks and Armenians settled below the site where a Byzantine imperial palace used to stand. Kontoscalion harbour in *Kumkapi* ('sand gate') silted up and was then used as land for a fishing village. Today there is an extremely nice fish market here. Beyond

it, in Ördekli Bakkal Sokak, you will find a host of charming taverns, amongst them Doyuran Lokantası and Kör Agop. *Doyuran Lokantası: daily midday–1am | Ördekli Bakkal Sok. 10 | tel. 0212 5 17 24 26; Kör Agop: daily midday–1am | Ördekli Bakkal Sok. 7 | tel. 0212 517 23 34*

SAF ☺ (131 D4) (*ID 0*)

The city's only restaurant specialising in raw vegetables is in the north, above Bebek. Vegetarians and vegans come here for the exclusively organic food, which is heated to a maximum temperature of 48 degrees Celsius. *Saf* (the name means 'pure') uses no wheat, meat or dairy products. *Daily 8am–1am | Cumhuriyet Cad. 4–8 (in Club Sporium behind the Mayadrom shopping centre) | Etiler-Akatlar | tel. 0212 2 82 79 46 | www. safrestaurant.com*

SOFYALI 9 (124 B4) (*ID H3*)

Decorated in the manner of a Greek taverna, this hip spot treats its lunchtime guests to plain home-style cooking, tasty and reasonably priced. In the evening chef Engin Usta puts on two dozen different kinds of starters, to be washed down with rakı, beer or wine. *Mon–Sat midday–1am | Asmalımescit, Sofyalı Sok. 9 | Beyoğlu-Tünel | tel. 0212 2 45 03 62*

TIKE LEVENT (131 D4) (*ID 0*)

İstanbul's classiest kebab joint, near the Metro and Akmerkez shopping centre. The owners come from Adana. If you come here, don't fail to try *cezerye* – a sweet treat made from nuts and carrots. *Daily | Haci Adil Cad. 4 | Aralık 1 (Levent) | tel. 0212 2 81 88 71 | www.tike.com.tr*

INSIDER TIP ▶ YAKUP 2 (124 B4) (*ID H3*)

There is probably not a single writer or journalist in İstanbul who hasn't joined in a drinking session here. Yakup Arslan

Decades of delicious food: Tarihi Sultanahmet Köftecisi

gives his customers a send-off long after midnight by ringing bells. Excellent İstanbul starters, good meat dishes from the grill. *Closed Sun | Tünel | Asmalı Mescit Sok. 35 | Beyoğlu | tel. 0212 2 49 29 25*

RESTAURANTS: BUDGET

ARMADA (124 B4) *(ᗰ H3)*
Right on İstiklal Caddesi, between the Russian and Swedish consulates, this self-service restaurant offers a wide range of meat, fish and vegetable dishes in good quality and at reasonable prices, which explains its popularity. *Daily 11am–10pm | İstiklal Cad. 231/B | Beyoğlu-Tünel | tel. 0212 2 49 79 27*

BAYA (124 C3) *(ᗰ J2)*
Baya is a Turkish-Mexican eatery with a retro ambience in the antiques district below İstiklal Caddesi. Whatever you order, from a Mexican breakfast to a good hamburger or a late-night margarita, you can be sure of getting a generous serving! *Daily | Ağahamam Sok. 29 | Çukurcuma-Taksim | tel. 0212 2 52 34 28*

BUHARA (129 D4) *(ᗰ H6)*
At the tourist end of the old quarter, by the Grand Bazaar. Good Turkish food is the order of the day. *Daily | Nuruosmaniye Cad. 27 | Cağaloğlu | tel. 0212 5 27 51 33*

INSIDER TIP ▶ CUMHURIYET MEYHA-NESI (124 B–C2) *(ᗰ J2)*
The city's most famous Turkish tavern, not least because the founder of the republic, Kemal Atatürk, liked to come here to down a rakı – at least that's the story doing the rounds in İstanbul. *Daily | Balık Pazarı | Sahne Sok. 47 | Beyoğlu | tel. 0212 2 43 64 06*

DUBB INDIAN ☙ (129 D4–5) *(ᗰ H7)*
Indian cuisine near Hagia Sophia: on the terrace you can gaze at the sea while drinking chai tea with aromatic spices. Food served until 11.30pm! *Daily | İncili Çavuş Sok. 10 | Sultanahmet | tel. 0212 5 13 73 08*

EFULI (125 D1) *(ᗰ K1)*
An address for breakfast, lunch or an evening meal; alongside dishes from the grill they also serve Viennese-style chicken. Clean, unpretentious and good. *Daily from 6.30am | Elmadağ | Cumhuriyet Cad. 12 | Taksim | tel. 0212 2 25 69 54*

KANAAT LOKANTASI ★ (131 D5) *(ᗰ O)*
Near where the Bosphorus ferries dock discover what may be the oldest eatery in İstanbul, known for excellent meals made to old Turkish recipes. As this is the religious quarter of Üsküdar, no alcohol is served. The service is restrained but friendly. No credit cards. *Daily | Selmanipak Cad. 9 | Üsküdar | tel. 0216 3 41 54 44*

KAPALIÇARŞI HAVUZLU LOKANTA (128 C4) *(ᗰ G6)*
In this restaurant by the Grand Bazaar you get a good lunch. Traditional food,

with an emphasis on aubergine dishes, and a quiet atmosphere. *Lunchtime only, closed Sun | Gami Çelebi Sok. 3 (next to the post office) | Kapalıçarşı | tel. 0212 5 27 33 46*

INSIDER TIP ▶ KARAKÖY LOKANTASI
(124 C5) (*𝄞 J4*)

This restaurant opposite the customs office on the harbour is housed in the rooms of what used to be the Estonian consulate. At lunchtime tasty and cheap daily specials are on the menu. In the evening the place morphs into a typical rakı tavern, but without loud music. The starters on their own (İstanbul cuisine) are very filling, but the vegetable and lamb dishes are also highly recommended. *Mon–Sat midday–4pm and 6pm–midnight | Kemankes Cad. 37 A | Karaköy | tel. 0212 2 92 44 55 | www.karakoy lokantasi.com*

KATIBIM ☙ (131 D5) (*𝄞 0*)

İstanbul residents love to come here for all sorts of kebab. The view from the Asian shore to the historic peninsula is terrific. *Daily | Şemsipaşa Sahil Yolu 53 | Üsküdar | tel. 0216 3 10 90 80*

NATURE AND PEACE ☺ (124 C2) (*𝄞 J2*)

Fresh vegetable dishes. The vegetarian menus are a snip at around £ 8. Small and clean. *Daily | İstiklal Cad. Büyük Parmakkapı Sok. 21 | Beyoğlu | tel. 0212 2 52 86 09*

PIZZERIA PIDO'S (125 E2) (*𝄞 K2*)

A reliable pizzeria furnished in bistro style with a good range of wines not far from Taksim Square. The speciality is pizza *melanzane* with aubergines. In summer it's great to sit in the garden. *Daily | Dünya Sağlık Sok. 15 | Gümüşsuyu | Taksim | tel. 0212 2 49 40 40*

TARIHI SULTANAHMET KÖFTECISI
(129 D4) (*𝄞 H7*)

For over 80 years the menu and quality of the *köfte lokantası* opposite the Blue Mosque have remained constant. Meatballs don't taste as good as this anywhere else. *Daily | Divanyolu Cad. 12/A | Sultanahmet | tel. 0212 5 13 14 38*

TEA GARDENS & CO.

INSIDER TIP ▶ BEBEK KAHVE ☙
(131 D4) (*𝄞 0*)

A coffee house with lots of character right by the sea, next to the Bebek Mosque, and a popular haunt of students from the nearby Bosphorus University. You can sit here with all the time in the world to watch what's happening on the water or just read a book. The branch of Starbucks next door has a pleasant timber terrace by the sea. *Daily | Bebek Camii Yanı | Bebek*

ÇINILI KÖŞK (129 E4) (*𝄞 J6*)

An oasis of peace and quiet: rest your weary legs after paying a visit to the Topkapı Palace or the Archaeological Museum in a delightful garden. *Tue–Sun 9am–6pm | by the Archaeological Museum, accessible only from the museum | Sultanahmet*

MODA ÇAY BAHÇESI ★ ☙
(131 D5) (*𝄞 0*)

Tea garden situated on a promontory opposite the historic peninsula. Young and old sit under the trees here in summer and winter alike to take in the sea view. An ideal place to get an impression of İstanbul's urban life. Behind the tea garden is a large children's playground, and you can keep an eye on it from your table. *Daily, in summer till midnight, in winter closing earlier | Devriye Sok. 7 | Moda*

SHOPPING

Photo: Grand Bazaar

CITY **WHERE TO START?**

In İstanbul traders are flourishing wherever you look. Alongside a traditional bazaar the Nişantaşı quarter above Taksim Square is a good area for a proper shopping spree. Extremely swish boutiques and fashion outlets are concentrated on famous streets such as **Abdi İpekçi Caddesi. Bağdat Caddesi** on the Asian side along the Sea of Marmara is the next-best alternative. And finally, the big shopping centres in İstanbul are places where you can find absolutely everything, from a hairpin to clothes.

In İstanbul everyone can buy what they are looking for. Discover centuries-old oriental markets and modern shopping districts.

For jewellery, carpets and traditional crafts, head for the historic peninsula north of Sultanahmet. The *Kapalı Çarşı* Grand Bazaar should be on every visitor's list, even if you don't want to buy anything. In the *Mısır Çarşısı* Spice Bazaar hundreds of different spices and medicinal herbs are on sale.

As gold is cheaper in Turkey than in the EU states, jewellery is a favourite purchase for visitors to İstanbul. Gold is traded in three categories: bracelets, for example, are 22-carat gold. The most popular items have 18 to 16 carats. White gold, *beyaz altın*, is not commonly sold,

Oriental bazaars and modern malls – there's
a long tradition of shopping in İstanbul

but there is a huge range of precious stones, especially diamonds, *elmas*, and cut diamonds, *pırlanta*.

Old calligraphy, engravings and photographs can be found in the book bazaar and the many antique shops in Beyoğlu. If you are interested in an expensive item, you can certainly bargain – make price comparisons rather than just relying on your gut feeling.

The district for buying carpets and kelims is in and around the Grand Bazaar: kelims are woven carpets as distinct from

knotted carpets. The best carpets are those with the most knots per square inch. The most expensive are *Hereke*, made of silk, while *Bergama, Konya, Uşak* and *Kayseri* are among the highest-quality carpets made from knotted cotton and treated with natural dyes. When it comes to patterned kelims, size and colour play an important part. Kelims whose colours come from chemical aniline dyes should not get wet, as the colours will then run. Most dealers will send a carpet to your home at no extra

Books about the sea:
Denizler Bookstore

Nişantaşı and along Bağdat Caddesi, but also in *Teşvikiye*, *Şişli* and *Etiler* on the European side. The people of İstanbul have taken in a big way to covered shopping malls with cafés, fast-food restaurants, children's play areas and multiplex cinemas. Along the Metro line between Taksim Square and Levent one shopping centre after another has opened up (*daily 10am–10pm*).

BOOKS NEW & SECOND-HAND

OLD BOOK BAZAAR (SAHAFLAR ÇARŞI) (128 C4) (*ᗄ G6*)
Second-hand bookstalls set up around the Grand Bazaar more than a century ago. Here you can buy old books, manuscripts, engravings and miniatures at fair prices. *Daily 9am–8pm | at the entrance to the Grand Bazaar | Beyazıt*

ARTRIUM (124 B4) (*ᗄ H3*)
One of the city's most attractive second-hand bookshops is situated inconspicuously in the arcade opposite the upper entrance to the Tünel railway. At Artrium you will find, among other things, fine, genuine (and therefore not exactly cheap!) miniatures and cards, as well as all sorts of affordable bits and bobs to take back home. *Mon–Sat 9am–7pm | Tünel Geçidi 7 | Beyoğlu-Tünel | www.artrium.com.tr*

INSIDER TIP DENIZLER BOOKSTORE (124 B3) (*ᗄ H3*)
Everything and anything connected with the sea: from novels to guidebooks for divers and marine charts. The owner is a passionate collector of all things maritime. Don't fail to come and take a look! *Mon–Sat 10am–8pm | İstiklal Cad. 199 A | Beyoğlu | www.denizlerkitabevi.com*

charge. If you want to take it back with you, get a receipt to present at customs when you depart.

There are modern shopping streets with cafés and little restaurants not only in

ANTIQUES

INSIDER TIP ▶ RAFFI PORTAKAL
(128 C4) (ᵭ G6)

From old paintings, calligraphy and Ottoman silver to expensive glass that graced the tables of viziers: this long-established auction house only stocks top-quality goods. *Mon–Sat 8am–7pm | Mim Kemal Öke Cad. 12 and 19 | Nişantaşı | www.rportakal.com*

SMALL ANTIQUES DEALERS
(ESKICILER) ★

Antiques are greatly sought-after and expensive in İstanbul. In the smaller and less exclusive shops, however, you have a reasonably good chance of laying your hands on some kind of little treasure. If you are looking for an unusual souvenir at an affordable price, you will surely find something to suit in one of these atmospheric little places. Don't forget to bargain! Here are two good addresses: *Çukurcuma Cad. | Beyoğlu* (124 C3) (ᵭ J3); *Büyük Hamam Sok. | Üsküdar* (131 D5) (ᵭ O)

BAZAARS

EGYPTIAN BAZAAR (MISIR ÇARŞISI)
(129 D2–3) (ᵭ H5)

The covered spice market in Eminönü (see the Sightseeing chapter) is the first place to go to for saffron, thyme and anything else along those lines. You can also buy caviar here. For a nice souvenir, look out for the hand-carved walking sticks made in villages in the forests of eastern Turkey. *Mon–Sat 9am–7pm | Eminönü Meydanı*

ARASTA BAZAAR (ARASTA ÇARŞISI)
(129 E5) (ᵭ J7)

This little market complex is home not only to the Byzantine Mosaic Museum but also to lots of little stores that offer Ottoman craft products and carpets. *Daily 9am–8pm | Sultanahmet | www.arastabazaar.com*

GRAND BAZAAR (KAPALI ÇARŞI)
(128 C4) (ᵭ G6)

Jewellery, leather goods, collectors' items made of meerschaum, hookahs, icons and souvenirs of every kind – at the Grand Bazaar (see the Sightseeing chapter) you can buy all these things and much more. And even if you don't find what you wanted, a walk around this enormous oriental market is an experience you'll not forget in a hurry. *Mon–Sat 8.30am–7pm| Beyazı*

DELICATESSEN

INSIDER TIP ▶ BEBEK BADEM EZMESI
(131 D4) (ᵭ O)

To purchase some excellent Turkish delicatessen such as marzipan rolls or

---

★ Antiques dealers
The vintage and antiques shops in Çukurcuma and Üsküdar are definitely worth a visit → p. 75

★ İznik Foundation
Beautiful ceramics made according to old Ottoman craft techniques and patterns → p. 76

★ Kanyon
İstanbul's best and most varied range of modern shopping outlets → p. 78

★ Şişko Osman
No-one in İstanbul knows more about carpets than 'Fat Osman' → p. 79

MARCO POLO HIGHLIGHTS

Traditional craftwork:
İznik fayence

find old Ottoman items such as *çesmi bülbül* – extremely refined glassware reminiscent of Venetian Murano glass. The goods are packed carefully for transport. Sales outlets exist all over the city, e.g.: *Tünel | İstiklal Cad. 314 | Beyoğlu* **(124 B3–4)** *(⚑ H3)*; *in northern İstanbul: daily 10am–10pm | Büyükdere Cad. | Maslak* **(131 D3)** *(⚑ 0) | www.sisecam.com*

SIR ÇİNİ **(124 B4)** *(⚑ H3)*

This studio for tiles and ceramics was founded by artist Sadullah Cekmece. It is a source for fine, hand-made Turkish and Ottoman objects such as vases, plates and bowls. **INSIDER TIP** Hand-painted ceramic plaques are sold at reasonable prices as framed one-off items. *Mon–Sat 9am–8pm | Serdar-ı Ekrem Sok. 38/1 | Galata | Beyoğlu | www.sircini.com*

FASHION & SHOES

BETA

The brothers Ercan and Taner Ikiisik started to make shoes in a small workshop in Levent. Today they produce 1500 pairs every day for domestic sales and for export. The style is comfortable, casual and robust, using genuine leather. *Daily 10am–7pm | İstiklal Cad. 69 | Beyoğlu-Taksim* **(124 C2)** *(⚑ J2)*; *Tunaman Çarşışı, Şakayık Sok. 47 | Nişantaşı* **(131 D4)** *(⚑ 0) | www.betashoes.com*

BEYMEN

This high-end Turkish brand of clothing has made its name with fine fabrics and classical design. You can also buy fashion from international brands at the outlet. *Daily 10am–10pm, outlet daily 10am–7.30pm | Akmerkez | Nispetiye Cad. Etiler* **(131 D4)** *(⚑ 0)*; *Abdi Ipekci Cad. 23/1 | Nişantaşı* **(131 D4)** *(⚑ 0)*; *Adnan Kahveci Cad. 116 | Ferahevler | Tarabya* **(131 D3)** *(⚑ 0) | www.beymen.com.tr*

almond sweets, it's worth taking a trip up the Bosphorus. *Daily 9.30am–8pm | Cevdet Paşa Cad. 238/1 | Bebek*

CRAFTS

İZNIK FOUNDATION ★
(131 D4) *(⚑ 0)*

In its workshops south of İstanbul, at the place where this craft originated, this foundation once again sells the beautifully painted faiences used to decorate, for example, the Blue Mosque. The product range runs from a dinner service to an ashtray. *Mon–Fri 8.30am–6pm, Sat 10am–5pm | Öksüz Çocuk Sok. 17 | Kuruçeşme | www.iznik.com*

INSIDER TIP PAŞABAHÇE

The state-run glass manufactories make high-class products from glass, earthenware and porcelain at very low prices. Alongside modern designs you will

BUTIK KATIA (124 C2) (*m H3*)

This hat shop in one of the oldest arcades in Pera has been in business since 1956. The Greek proprietor, Madame Katia, represents the second generation, as her mother founded the shop. You can get a hat made to measure here, even at short notice. *Mon–Sat 10am–6pm | İstiklal Cad. 37, Danisment (Hacopulo) arcade | Beyoğlu*

DERIMOD

The leading brand in Turkish leather clothing also makes shoes and handbags. *Daily 10am–8pm | Bağdat Cad. 303 | Kadıköy (131 D6) (m 0); in the Akmerkez shopping centre | Nispetiye Cad. | Etiler (131 D4) (m 0); outlet: Büyükdere Cad. 59 | Maslak (131 D3) (m 0) | www.derimod.com.tr*

DERISHOW (0) (*m 0*)

Derishow produce high-quality leather jackets, and their store also sells textile fashion in good quality with designs that reveal originality. *Daily 9.30am–7.30pm | Fulya | Ihlamur Cad., Yesilcimen Sok. 17 | Beşiktaş | www.derishow.com.tr*

VAKKO (131 D4) (*m 0*)

The old-established base of Jewish-Turkish fashion designer Vitali Hakko in Nişantaşı, split up into several shops. *Daily 10am–8pm | Abdi Ipekci Cad. 31 (men), 37 (wedding dresses), 38 (women) and 48 (shoes and handbags) | www.vakko.com.tr*

INSIDER TIP YARGICI (131 D4) (*m 0*)

Attractive fashion for women made by the female designer Neslihan Yargici at affordable prices: delicate colours, excellent woollen and linen fabrics, classically chic. Handbags, shoes, jewellery and accessories are also available here. *Mon–Sat 9.30am–7.30pm, Sun 1pm–6pm | Valikonağı Cad. 30 | Nişantaşı | www.yargici.com.tr*

ORGANIC PRODUCTS

AMBAR ☺ (124 B3) (*m H2*)

This store for natural and organic products has been operating in Beyoğlu since 2001 and is now well established in İstanbul. Its natural products such as cosmetics containing apricots or olive and almond oil are extremely popular; spice mixtures and natural soaps make a nice present that's easy to take home. *Daily 10am–8pm | Kallavi Sok. 6 | Beyoğlu | www.nuhunambari.com*

BÜNSA ☺ (124 B–C2) (*m J2*)

An exemplary health-food shop: in addition to spices and air-dried fruit you can also buy Black Sea honey here. *Daily 10am–7pm | Balık Pazari 26 | Galatasaray*

JENNIFER'S HAMAM ☺ (129 E5) (*m J7*)

Canadian Jennifer Gaudet, the only female owner of a store in the Arasta Bazaar, arrived in İstanbul after teaching English in Thailand for seven years. Now she sells garments and textiles for bathing, and body-care products. She looks closely at certificates of origin and buys exclusively organic products. *April–Sept daily 9am–10.30pm, Oct–March 9am–7.30pm | Arasta Bazaar 135 | Sultanahmet | www.jennifershamam.com*

JEWELLERY

ANTIKART (124 C2) (*m J2*)

There are several shops in this arcade of jewellers. This store specialises in replicas of Trojan and Hittite jewellery. *Mon–Sat 10am–9.30pm, Sun midday–9.30pm | İstiklal Cad. 207 | Atlas Kuyumcular Çarşısı 32 | Beyoğlu*

SHOPPING MALLS

CEVAHİR BEDESTENİ (128 C4) (𝖒 G6)
The 'old bazaar' at the heart of the Grand Bazaar houses many jewellers' stores, which sell antique silver as a main line of business. In the alleyways close by you will also find gold jewellery. *Mon–Sat 8.30am–7pm | Kapalıçarşı | Beyazıt | www.kapalicarsi.org.tr*

URART (0) (𝖒 0)
Here young avant-garde Turkish designers offer works made in silver, gold and other materials for sale. Replicas of ancient Anatolian and Trojan jewellery. *Mon–Sat 9am–7pm | Abdi İpekçi Cad. 18 | Nişantaşı | www.urart.com.tr*

SHOPPING MALLS

AKMERKEZ (131 D4) (𝖒 0)
This shopping centre in the north of the city is one of the swankiest places for indoor shopping. The 140 stores under its roof include shops selling lots of international labels as well as products by Turkish designers, an art gallery, cafés and restaurants. *Daily 10am–10pm | Nispetiye Cad. | Etiler | by Metro from Taksim to Levent, then take a taxi | www.akmerkez.com.tr*

İSTANBUL SAPPHIRE (131 D3) (𝖒 0)
Thanks to its interior gardens, this 856-foot skyscraper has been hailed as an 'ecological wonder' – unfortunately everything is tucked away behind glass. In a shopping centre on the lower storeys you can buy interesting Ottoman and Islamic-style souvenirs, e. g. replicas of old silver services and porcelain. A lift whizzes you up to a 🔭 viewing deck with an awesome view of İstanbul. *Daily 10am–10pm | admission to the viewing platform approx. £ 6.50 | Büyükdere Cad. 4 | Levent | Metro-Station Levent | www.istanbulsapphire.com*

İSTİNYE PARK (131 D3) (𝖒 0)
With 300 shops, including stores for luxury brands from all around the world, this shopping centre, opened above İstinye on the Bosphorus in 2007, is a magnet for İstanbul's high society. A market for organic products rounds off the range of goods. *Daily 10am–10pm | İstinye Bayırı Cad. 73 | Sarıyer | shuttle bus midday–2pm from Oto Sanayi Metro station | www.istinyepark.com*

KANYON ★ ● (131 D4) (𝖒 0)
Over 160 shops on four floors: from Dior to Harvey Nichols and Max Mara, you'll find dozens of fashion brands here. A bookshop (Remzi), cafés and restaurants (e. g. Wagamama) and a multiplex cinema (Mars) add to the attractions at Kanyon, which is in itself an architectural marvel and the most beautiful shopping centre in İstanbul. *Daily 10am–10pm |*

LOW BUDGET

▶ *Tombak* **(122 C3)** *(𝖒 J3) (daily 10am–8pm | Faikpaşa Yok. 34, Çukurcuma | Beyoğlu-Taksim)* is chock-a-block to the ceiling with antiques and flea-market goods.

▶ Swimming things and bikinis in the very best quality are sold at *Ayyıldız* **(128 C4)** *(𝖒 0)*. *Daily 9am–8pm | Atiye Sok. 8 | Teşvikiye | www.ayyildiz.com.tr*

▶ Underwear by the Kom brand can be had cheaply at the *outlet* **(0)** *(𝖒 0)*. *Daily 9am–7pm | Güvenç Sok. 15-17/A | Bomonti-Şişli | www.kom.com.tr*

*Büyükdere Cad. 185 | Levent | tel. 0212
3 53 53 00 | Dördüncü Levent and Taksim
Metro stations | www.kanyon.com.tr*

CARPETS & FABRICS

ETHNICON (128 C4) (*𝄞 G6*)

Ethnicon is a company with an original
specialisation: INSIDER TIP patchwork
kelims, sewn together from pieces of old
carpets. The results are wonderful and
surprising, and guarantee pleasure for
years to come if you take one back home.

select items, from bed linen and swimming things to top-class Turkish coffee.
She also takes care to sourcing products
such as olive oil and olive soaps from
suppliers who certify organic produc-
tion. *Akaretler, Şair Nedim Bey Cad. 11 |
Beşiktaş | www.haremlique.com*

ŞİSKO OSMAN ★ (128 C4) (*𝄞 G6*)

'Fat Osman's' is one of the best addresses
in the Grand Bazaar for expensive carpets. On his website Osman explains the
motifs on his wares. *Mon–Sat 8.30am–*

Akmerkez has a reputation as one of Europe's very best shopping centres

*Mon–Sat 8.30am–7pm | Takkeciler Sok.
58–60 | Kapalı Çarşı | www.ethnicon.com*

INSIDER TIP HAREMLIQUE ☺ (131 D4) (*𝄞 0*)

Caroline Koç, née Giraud, is descended
from Levantines, i.e. Europeans who
lived in the eastern Mediterranean from
the 18th century. Her family used to run
a textile business, and she still keeps up
this tradition with her own design brand:
Haremlique. In her shop, which bears the
name of the women's quarters in an Ottoman palace, you will find only the most

*7pm | Halıcılar Cad. 49 | Zincirli Han 15 |
Kapalı Çarşı | www.siskoosman.com*

SIVASLI YAZMACISI ☺ (128 C4) (*𝄞 G6*)

Colourfully patterned printed cotton fabrics from eastern Anatolia are on sale in
this long-established shop in the Grand
Bazaar. Hand-woven, embroidered and
crocheted items can also be had. All
products are made using exclusively nat-
ural dyes. *Daily 8.30am–7pm | Yağlıkçılar
Sok. 57 | Kapalı Çarşı*

ENTERTAINMENT

🏙 WHERE TO START?

The city's nightspots are clustered on both shores of the Bosphorus and in Beyoğlu. To enjoy a classy sundowner, the European side of the water is the right choice. In **Ortaköy** and **Kuruçeşme** there are countless bars and taverns around the first Bosphorus bridge, and you don't need to be young to have a good time in trendy locations such as Reina and Sortie. **Bebek** is another district with some cool watering holes, and its plus point is that you can have a good meal here too. In **Beyoğlu** the atmosphere in the clubs is more relaxed and the clientele is somewhat younger.

İstanbul never sleeps – from a long, leisurely meal in one of the excellent restaurants on the Bosphorus to the obligatory early-morning soup in one of the places that stay open 24 hours a day, you will find 1001 ways of spending an unforgettable evening in this city.

İstiklal Caddesi and the side streets running off it appeal mainly to an avantgarde crowd. If you want something high-class, it's worth making a trip to Levent or down to the Bosphorus. Kadife Sokak in Kadıköy has something for every taste and isn't too hard on the pocket. Most drinking establishments (they generally call themselves bars) are pretty noisy, and live music is played in many of them. The ☀ roof bars of

Photo: Babylon music club

There's more to İstanbul's nightlife than belly dancing: the options run from open-air clubbing and cool bars to jazz in smoky basements

the big hotels such as the *Conrad, Inter-Continental* and *Etap Marmara* are also worth considering, because of course they give you a great view of İstanbul by night.

The belly-dance shows of the *gazinos* on İstiklal Caddesi are mediocre and overpriced. Another expensive night out, but with quality to match the price tag, is the 'Turkish Night' in the Galata Tower.

Most places will accept credit cards, but for any eventualities it's wise to have cash with you! In the bars with music and dance clubs you either pay an admission charge (from about £ 6.50 including a free drink) or a fixed price for the first drink, regardless of whether you opt for whisky or mineral water. There are minders on the door at all clubs and many of the higher-end bars to keep out undesirables. Be aware that they usually don't let in unaccompanied men. To get home afterwards, the sensible course is to hail a taxi, or better still get the porter to call one for you – that's the safer option.

Plenty of atmosphere
at Bilsak Beşinci Kat

BARS & PUBS

INSIDER TIP **ANJELIQUE** (131 D4) (*Ø O*)
This in-bar on the Bosphorus is a rendezvous for well-groomed people who want to sip a cocktail and listen to some popular hits. You are expected to dress smartly here. From 6pm until midnight warm Mediterranean-style dishes are served here. *Daily 6pm–4am | free admission | Muallim Naci Cad. Salhane Sok. 10/2 | Ortaköy*

BEBEK BAR ★ ☆ (131 D4) (*Ø O*)
In the 1980s this was one of the best bars in the world. It's still a great place to try, as the well-frequented bar of the old-established hotel *Bebek* on the Bosphorus is the ideal choice for an evening drink. From the terrace the view of the bay of Bebek is fantastic. But be warned: this is a high-end joint! *Daily 5pm–1am | Cevdet Paşa Cad. 34 | Bebek | www.bebek hotel.com.tr*

BILSAK BEŞINCI KAT ☆
(125 D3) (*Ø J2*)
From the 'Fifth Floor' of an alternative arts centre you get a wonderful view of the Bosphorus. *Daily 10am–2am | Sıraselviler Cad., Soğancı Sok. 7 | Cihangir | www.5kat.com*

JAMES JOYCE IRISH PUB/
THE IRISH CENTRE (124 C2) (*Ø J2*)
If you like Irish music, then it's on tap without interruption here, and at the weekends live concerts are held. Pub food is served, and the customers are not restricted to the local Irish community. *Daily 1pm–2am | İstiklal Cad., Balo Sok. 26 | Beyoğlu | www.theirishcenter.com*

KÜÇÜK BEYOĞLU (124 C2) (*Ø J2*)
'Little Beyoğlu' consists of four pubs that form a drinking alley of their own in the entertainment quarter. *La Rambla, Fabrika, Paralel* and *Last Pub* are under the same ownership, and provide space for 900 guests inside, and a further 300 outdoors. *Daily 10am–2am | Yeşilçam Sok. | Beyoğlu-Taksim | tel. 0212 21 75 99*

LINE (124 C2) (*Ø J2*)
Thanks to its minimalist furnishings, this bar manages to distinguish itself from the other smoke-filled dives in Beyoğlu. At the weekend rock bands provide live music. *Daily midday–4am | Büyükparmakkapı Sok. 14 A/B | Beyoğlu | www.linebar.com*

LOKAL MEYDAN (124 B4) (*Ø H3*)
You're unlikely to miss this bar slap bang on Tünel Square. During the day things are fairly quiet, while in the evening both storeys turn into dance floors. Ideal as a place to meet. *Daily 11am–2am | İstiklal Cad. 186 a | Tünel (Beyoğlu-Taksim) | tel. 0212 2 45 40 28*

THE NORTH SHIELD

Drink cold beer while watching football on a big screen, or enjoy an early-evening aperitif or a cognac by the fire: this is a chain of English pubs, with several branches in İstanbul, e.g. in Beyoğlu and Sultanahmet. *Sun–Thu 11am–1am, Fri–Sat 11am–2am | Asmalı Mescit, Meşrutiyet Cad. 55 (in the entrance to the Palazzo Donizetti Hotel) | Beyoğlu (124 B3) (ⓜ H3); Ebusuud Cad. 2 | Sultanahmet (129 D3) (ⓜ H6) | www.the northshield.com*

SARDUNYA ☼ (125 D4) (ⓜ H4)

Sardunya is situated on the Bosphorus at the old harbour of Karaköy. The circular outdoor bar makes a nice spot for a drink and a chat, as it's quiet and cosy here. *Only in summer, daily 7pm–1am | Meclis-i Mebusan Cad. 22 | Salıpazarı (Karaköy) | www.sardunyafindikli.com*

TOUCHDOWN (131 D4) (ⓜ O)

This popular bar is just what you need to recover from a shopping tour with a drink. *Daily 10am–0.30am | Abdi Ipekçi Cad. 61/11 (Reasürans Çarşısı) | Teşvikiye | www.touchdown.com.tr*

INSIDER TIP URBAN (124 C3) (ⓜ J2)

The owner is a jazz-lover who brought back a big collection of CDs from Switzerland, where he lived for many years. The stylish bar on two levels gets packed in the evening. The food is excellent, and there is plenty of space outside for smokers. *Daily 9am (as a café) to 1am | Kartal Sok. 6 A | Beyoğlu-Galatasaray | tel. 0212 2 52 13 25 | www.urbanbeyoglu.com*

W LOUNGE (131 D4) (ⓜ O)

This bar is in one of the fine houses on Akaretler in Beşiktaş, a row of buildings dating from the 19th century. The unique feature of W Lounge is that it stays open 7 days a week round the clock! *Süleyman Seba Cad. 22 | Akaretler (Beşiktaş) | tel. 0212 3 81 21 21*

BELLY DANCING

GALATA KULESI NIGHTCLUB ☼
(124 B4) (ⓜ H4)

Belly dancing, traditional dances and singers, with a good view of the old part of town thrown in. Touristy and pricey. *Daily 8pm–2am | Hendek Cad. Beyoğlu | www.galatatower.net*

KERVANSARAY (125 D1) (ⓜ K1)

This nightclub near the Hilton Hotel in the Taksim Square district has been going since 1949 and is truly an institution on İstanbul's night scene. The best Turkish belly dancers launched their careers here, and it is still the place to come if you want to see INSIDER TIP the city's most talented belly dancers. Other forms of entertainment are on offer too,

---

★ Bebek Bar
Quiet, classic bar in the grand old hotel of the same name with a great sea view → p. 82

★ Reina
Where *tout le monde* comes together on the Bosphorus. Things really get going here after midnight → p. 84

★ Hayal Kahvesi
Turkish rock and blues – in summer guests dance beneath the starry sky → p. 86

★ Nardis
This club by the Galata Tower is the best address for jazz music in all İstanbul → p. 87

MARCO POLO HIGHLIGHTS

BOSPHORUS TOURS

including Caucasian folklore and some good entertainers. With its high ceilings and classical ambience, this is one of the classier nightspots in town. Diners get a set menu with starters, kebab, dessert, coffee and two alcoholic drinks for £ 50. Reservations and low-key evening dress are the order of the day. *Cumhuriyet Cad. 52 A | Taksim | tel. 0212 2 47 16 30 | www. kervansarayistanbul.com*

SULTANA'S (125 D1) (*ΩΩ K1*)

'Dinner and 1001 Nights Show' is the name of the programme that's on every night here. Guests have to book a table in advance by phone. In the restaurant you get a choice between various set menus or à la carte. The show, which is mainly aimed at tourists, consists of belly dancing, diverse folklore, singers and other acts. Sultana's is conveniently located close to Taksim Square. *Cumhuriyet Cad. 40 (between Taksim Square and the Interconti Hotel) | Taksim | tel. 0212 2 19 39 04 | Metro Taksim | www.sultanas-nights.com*

BOSPHORUS TOURS

In İstanbul you can take a trip on a motor launch on the Bosphorus in daylight hours or in the evening. The tours with snacks and soft drinks start on the European side in *Eminönü* behind the Galata Bridge on the Golden Horn and in *Beşiktaş* next to the ferry quays. On the Asian side you can get aboard in *Kadıköy* behind the small historic quay and in *Üsküdar* too. A single ticket costs less than £ 5.

LÜFER TOURS (131 D4) (*ΩΩ O*)

The biggest operator, with 15 boats plying the Bosphorus, from a romantic barge to steamers for excursions. The evening tour starts at 7.30pm in *Bebek* and finishes at midnight. You can also embark in *Beylerbeyi* on the Asian side. *From approx. £ 16 | Tasocagi Mevkii Balabandere 5 | Istinye | tel. 0212 2 29 64 64 | www.lufer.com.tr*

DANCE CLUBS

BLACKK ✂ (131 D4) (*ΩΩ O*)

Popular disco on the Bosphorus with a superb view across the water, extremely chic and crowded at weekends. It's a good idea to make a booking, so the gentlemen on the door let you in. *Daily 10.30pm–4am | Muallim Naci Cad. 71 | Kuruçeşme | tel. 0212 2 36 72 56 | www.blackk.net*

CLUB 29 ✂ (131 E3) (*ΩΩ O*)

The rich and beautiful get together here in a kind of Hadrian's villa with a restaurant, disco and pool bar right by the Bosphorus. *June–Sept daily 10am–6pm, 9pm–4am | Pasabahçe Yolu 24 | Çubuklu | www.club29.com*

CRYSTAL (131 D4) (*ΩΩ O*)

Trendy club with house and techno music, laid on by İstanbul's best-known DJs. Admission incl. one drink £ 15. *Thu 11pm–4am, Sat, Sun 0.30am–6.30am | Muallim Naci Cad. 65 | Ortaköy | www. clubcrystal.org*

MOJO (124 C2) (*ΩΩ J2*)

A rock bar where live music can be heard from time to time. *Daily 7pm–4am | Büyükparmakkapı Sok. 26 | Beyoğlu | www.mojomusic.org*

REINA ★ ✂ (131 D4) (*ΩΩ O*)

Located directly on the Bosphorus, this huge, hip club has 10 different bars, cafés and restaurants on site. In summer Reina is the focal point of İstanbul's nightlife. No admission without advance booking! *May–Oct daily 6pm–3am | Muallim Naci Cad. 44 | Kuruçeşme | www.reina.com.tr*

This İstanbul feeling: on balmy summer nights you can sit under the stars at Reina

SORTIE ※ (131 D4) (*Ø O*)

Open-air club for a trendy crowd: £ 20 admission gets you a drink and a wonderful night beneath the stars. Jam-packed at weekends! *Daily 5.30pm–4am | Muallim Naci Cad. 54 | Kuruçeşme | www.sortie.com.tr*

SWITCH (124 B3) (*Ø H2*)

Club in Beyoğlu opposite the Odakule office block. Avant-garde music for the young generation. *Fri, Sat 11pm–4am | İstiklal Cad. Muammer Karaca Çık. 3 | Beyoğlu*

CINEMAS

Films are screened in the original version with Turkish subtitles. Alongside the multiplex cinemas there are still a few charming old picture palaces. You'll find the cinemas lined up along İstiklal Caddesi. Thursday is 'people's day' with admission reduced by 30 per cent.

MOVIEPLEX (131 D4) (*Ø O*)

A big modern cinema, where the latest films can always be seen. *Tickets approx. £ 5 | Nispetiye Cad. Melodi Pasajı 14 | Etiler*

MUSIC CLUBS

INSIDER TIP ▶ BABYLON (124 B4) (*Ø H3*)

Babylon is a pub and arts centre rolled into one. Concerts and non-mainstream theatre of high quality are staged here. During the İstanbul Jazz Festival the club is one of the main venues. Down-Beat magazine voted it one of the world's 100 best jazz clubs. *Tue–Sat 9.30pm–4am | Asmalımescıt, Şehbender Sok. 3 | Tünel | www.babylon-ist.com*

BALANS MUSIC & PERFORMANCE HALL (124 C2) (*Ø J2*)

Live music and concerts by Turkish and international singers and bands make up the programme here. It is an extremely popular club for the people of İstanbul. *Wed–Sat 9pm–4am | Galatasaray, Balo Sok. 22 (corner of Nevizade) | Beyoğlu | www.jollyjokerbalans.com*

EYLÜLIST (131 D4) (*Ø O*)

Come here if you want to get to know Turkish singer-songwriters. The ground floor is home to a café with a sea view, and upstairs is a bar. *Café daily 5pm–2am,*

Roxy is not just for partying, it's about making music too

programme 11.30pm–2.30am | 1 Cad. 64 A | Arnavutköy | www.eylulist.com

GHETTO (124 C2) (*Ø J2*)

The Turkish-American jazz saxophonist Ilhan Ersahin opened this music lounge in 2007 in Beyoğlu. World-class musicians take the stage here, but Ghetto is a club in the New York style rather than a concert hall. Thu–Sun 10pm–4.30am | Kalyoncu Kulluk Cad. 10 | Beyoğlu | www.ghettoist.com

HAYAL KAHVESI ⭐

In this traditional rock and blues bar in Beyoğlu various Turkish groups do their stuff. The beer is good, the music loud. In summer the branch on the Asian side, Çubuklu, opens for business, and guests can dance outdoors by the Bosphorus. Shuttle boats go there from İstinye. Beyoğlu: daily 9pm–4am, Büyükparmakkapı Sok. 19 (124 C2) (*Ø J2*); Çubuklu: daily midday–2am, café during the day, food served 7pm–

midnight, Fri, Sat live music 11pm–4am | Burunbahçe Mevkii Çubuklu (131 E3) (*Ø 0*) | www.hayalkahvesi.com.tr

İSTANBUL JAZZ CENTER (131 D4) (*Ø 0*)

One of the city's finest jazz clubs is up on the roof of the Radisson Hotel. As well as concerts the attractions here are an upmarket restaurant and a lovely garden for balmy evenings of jazz with international performers. An expensive night out! Daily 6pm–3am, Mon no live music | Ciragan Cad. 10 | Ortaköy | www.istanbuljazz.com

KEMANCI ROCK BAR (125 D2) (*Ø J2*)

There's live rock and pop here every night, with occasional non-mainstream theatre and other kinds of performances. The Kemanci Rock Bar is *the* bar for the alternative scene in İstanbul. On two floors, with disco. Daily 1pm–4am, disco 7.30pm–4am | Sıraselviler Cad. 69/1 | Taksim | www.kemanci.org

INSIDER TIP ► MIMI TAVERNA
(131 D4) (𝖨𝖨 0)

An institution loved not only by the Greeks, a taverna for uninhibited dancing and drinking. Greek music (often live) and very generous starters. *Tue–Sun 7pm–3am | 1. Cadde 85 | Arnavutköy | www.mimitaverna.com*

NARDİS ★ (124 B5) (𝖨𝖨 H4)

Renowned Turkish jazz musicians and foreign artists perform at this club by the Galata Tower. It's the ideal place for getting to know the İstanbul jazz scene and a highly recommended evening out. *Live music Sun–Thu 9.30pm–0.30am, Fri, Sat 11.30pm–1.30am | Kuledibi Sok. 14 | Galata | www.nardisjazz.com*

OLYMPIA WISH CLUB (124 B3) (𝖨𝖨 H2)

Baba Zula, Manga, Nev, Kurban: the famous alternative bands in İstanbul, who aim to make their music a synthesis of eastern and western sounds, can be heard live here. *Wed–Sat 9pm–4am | İstiklal Cad., Acar Sok. 2 | Beyoğlu*

ROXY/ROXANNE (125 D3) (𝖨𝖨 J2)

Party nights at the weekend, and Latin, blues or jazz on other days of the week. During festivals Turkish and foreign musicians take the stage. *Tue–Sat 8.30pm–4am | Sıraselviler Cad., Aslan Yatağı Sok. 13 | Taksim | www.roxy.com.tr*

THE HALL (124 C2) (𝖨𝖨 J2)

A leading venue in Beyoğlu with live sets and DJs. You don't have to be young here. *Fri, Sat 9pm–4am | Küçük Bayram Sok. 7 | Beyoğlu (Taksim) | tel. 0212 2 44 87 37*

OPERA & SHOWS

İŞSANAT (131 D4) (𝖨𝖨 0)

Since it was established in 1990 this arts centre under the roof of the twin towers of the İş Bank has seen lots of big nights. International stars as well as Turkish orchestras and soloists perform in the concert hall with its excellent acoustics. Tickets: *www.biletix.com. İş Sanat Kültür Merkezi | İş Kuleleri Levent | tel. 0212 3 16 10 83 | www.issanat.com.tr*

INSIDER TIP ► SÜREYYA (131 D5) (𝖨𝖨 0)

Built in 1927 by a patron of the arts named Süreyya Ilmen for the residents of the Asian shore of the city, the amazing charm of this opera house has been even more apparent since it was restored in 2008. It is the principal stage for opera and ballet performances in İstanbul. *Bahariye Cad. 29 | Kadıköy | tel. 0216 3 46 15 31 | www.sureyyaoperasi.org*

LOW BUDGET

► Hotel bars with a view across the city don't have to be expensive. At the long bar of the *Richmond Hotel* **(124 B3)** (𝖨𝖨 *H3)* (*daily 5pm–2am | Bar Leb-i Derya, İstiklal Cad. 445, 6th floor | Beyoğlu | tel. 0212 2 43 43 75*) you can drink grog for only £ 4.

► The cheapest beer in Beyoğlu (a half-litre of Efes for under £ 2) can be found in the little alley opposite the tram stop on Tünel Square **(124 B4)** (𝖨𝖨 *H3).* In winter too you can sit outside beneath heaters.

► At the concerts in the *Acik Hava Tiyatrosu* below Taksim Square **(125 D2)** (𝖨𝖨 *K2)*, the cheapest seats on the upper tiers of the open-air theatre cost only £8–9. Programme and tickets: *www.biletix.com*

WHERE TO STAY

In İstanbul you will find all categories of hotel, from luxurious to basic. Because there are so many rooms available, it's easy to book one even at short notice.

In Sultanahmet, the historic centre of the city, there are many beautifully restored smaller hotels that can be strongly recommended. They are run with a special permit from the ministry of tourism, which applies strict standards. The criteria range from warm water to satellite or cable TV for receiving foreign-language channels. For a fee, hotels are willing to arrange a pick-up at the airport. The luxury hotels put on special offers, including weekend trips and city tours. And if you choose accommodation on the Princes' Islands, you can expect peace and quiet. An overnight stay in İstanbul is no longer cheap, because this city is hip! Many hotels will give a discount of up to 40 per cent for internet bookings – see *www.istanbulhotels.com* to take advantage of this. Other hotels advertise higher prices on their websites than they actually charge when you book. It makes sense to phone and check what the price really is. And there's nothing wrong with bargaining!

HOTELS: EXPENSIVE

ANEMON GALATA (124 B5) (*M H4*)
This hotel is located right by the Galata Tower in a nicely restored old building, in the middle of all the action. It has a lovely terrace with a good restaurant. *7 suites, 23 rooms | Büyükhendek Cad. 5 |*

Whether in a luxury hotel on the Bosphorus or in an old wooden Ottoman villa – look forward to a wonderful night's sleep

Bereketzade Mahallesi | Beyoğlu | tel. 0212 2 93 23 43 | www.anemonhotels.com

BEBEK HOTEL ★ ☼ (131 D4) (*Ø 0*)

An exclusive address with a wonderful bar and terrace in the bay of Bebek. Originally the building belonged to a textile manufacturer from Bursa. In the 1950s he opened a hotel that was strongly oriented to a western style of life. The piano evenings in the bar are still legendary. The hotel lies right on the waterfront and has large rooms, nine of them with a sea view. *21 rooms | Cevdetpaşa Cad. 34 | Bebek | tel. 0212 3 58 20 00 | www.bebekhotel.com.tr*

LUSH HİP (125 D2) (*Ø K2*)

As trendy as it gets: in the Lush Hip every room is designed and furnished in a different style. This cool modern hotel is situated on Taksim Square, so it's advisable to book one of the quieter rooms at the back! *22 rooms | Sıraselviler Cad. 50 | Taksim-Beyoğlu | tel. 0212 2 43 95 95 | www.lushhiphotel.com*

THE MARMARA İSTANBUL

The Marmara Hotel has no less than three houses in İstanbul, offering good quality at affordable prices. Their

RICHMOND (124 B4) (*ⅅ H3*)

This hotel on İstiklal Caddesi, Beyoğlu's showcase avenue, is definitely part of the old, European Pera. A 19th-century

At the Empress Zoe you sleep in the historic quarter

INSIDER TIP 🌿 rooftop restaurants are especially popular. *The Marmara İstanbul: 410 rooms | Taksim Meydanı | Beyoğlu* **(125 D2)** *(ⅅ J2)* | *tel. 0212 2 51 46 49; The Marmara Pera: 202 rooms, 3 suites | Meşrutiyet Cad. | Tepebaşı, Beyoğlu* **(124 B3)** *(ⅅ H3)* | *tel. 0212 2 51 46 46; The Marmara Şişli: 107 rooms | Ortaklar Cad. 30 | Şişli* **(131 D4)** *(ⅅ 0)* | *tel. 0212 3 70 94 00 | www.themarmara hotels.com*

MIDTOWN (125 D2) (*ⅅ J2*)

The name says what you get: the Midtown is ideally situated, right in the middle of the city on Taksim Square. 🌿 Nine of the rooms have a lovely view of the Bosphorus. The atmosphere is modern, bright and friendly. *80 rooms | Lamartin Cad. 13 | Taksim | tel. 0212 3 61 67 67 | www.midtown-hotel.com*

façade conceals a hotel with all modern amenities. *101 rooms, 8 suites | İstiklal Cad. 227 | Beyoğlu | tel. 0212 2 52 54 60 | www.richmondhotels.com.tr*

YEŞİL EV ⭐ (129 E5) (*ⅅ J7*)

In the heart of the historic old quarter between Hagia Sophia and the Blue Mosque, this is a magnificent example of the restored buildings owned by the Turkish automobile club. It is a late 19th-century townhouse. The marvellously quiet courtyard with a fountain can be used by non-residents in search of refreshments. The rooms have been decorated and furnished in 19th-century style. *20 rooms, 1 pasha suite | Kabasakal Cad. 5 | Sultanahmet | tel. 0212 5 17 67 85 | www.istanbulyesilev.com*

HOTELS: MODERATE

AU PERA HOTEL
(124 B4) (*H2*)

This hotel opened in 2010 in a restored palais, centrally located opposite the former US consulate. The interiors have been designed to match the historic surroundings. Internet, satellite TV, air conditioning. *20 rooms, 3 suites | Meşrutiyet Cad. 97 | Tepebaşı-Beyoğlu | tel. 0212 2 92 30 90 | www.hotelaupera.com*

AYASOFYA KONAKLARİ ★
(129 E4) (*J7*)

In a little pedestrianised street between Hagia Sophia and the Topkapı Palace several old wooden houses have been restored to high standards and converted into a very pleasant and smart hotel. Guests have a view of the centuries-old walls of the Topkapı Palace. *56 rooms, 7 suites | Soğukçeşme Sok. | Sultanahmet | tel. 0212 5 13 36 60 | www.ayasofyapensions.com*

INSIDER TIP ► EMPRESS ZOE
(129 E5) (*J7*)

A superbly restored corner building with a lovely little courtyard that has been made into a private archaeological garden. From here you have a view of the ruins of the Ottoman hamam of Ishak Pasha, built in 1483. *25 rooms | Akbiyik Cad. 4/1 | Sultanahmet | tel. 0212 5 18 25 04 | www.emzoe.com*

INSIDER TIP ► KARİYE (122 B3) (*C3*)

This hotel is located a little outside the city centre. Its guests include many groups of pilgrims from Greece, who like to stay close to the Chora Church and the Greek Orthodox patriarchate. For those who can do without nightlife and are interested in exploring the Byzantine and Ottoman side of İstanbul's history, this is the ideal hotel. Under the same roof the *Restaurant Asitane* serves up some of the best Turkish cooking in the city. *27 rooms | Kariye Camii Sok. 6 | Edirnekapı | tel. 0212 5 34 84 14 | www.kariyeotel.com*

★ **Bebek Hotel**
With a bit of luck you'll bag a room with a view of the Bosphorus – and at night watch the sailing boats passing by. A dream → p. 89

★ **Yeşil Ev**
History all around: this elegant town house is located between Hagia Sophia and the Blue Mosque → p. 90

★ **Ayasofya Konaklari**
Several beautifully restored wooden houses in a side street by the wall of the seraglio → p. 91

★ **Merit Halki Palace**
This house on the Princes' Island of Heybeli is a true idyll between the sea and the pine woods, the ideal place for a few relaxing days → p. 92

★ **Pera Palace**
The Pera Palace is reliving old traditions by providing its guests with pure luxury in historic surroundings → p. 92

★ **Mina Hotel**
Central, comfortable and reasonably priced. The fantastic terrace restaurant is an inviting spot → p. 94

MARCO POLO HIGHLIGHTS

KYBELE (129 E4) (*m J7*)

At the heart of the old quarter, close to the main sights, this hotel has a small courtyard that is just right for passing a quiet hour or two. A wealth of antiques and an interesting collection of glass lamps adorn the interior. *16 rooms | Yerebatan Cad. 35 | Sultanahmet | tel. 0212 5 11 77 66 | www.kybele hotel.com*

MERIT HALKI PALACE ⭐ ☆

(0) (*m 0*)

If you want to treat yourself to something special, book a room with a balcony facing the sea in the Merit Halki Palace, where you will stay in style in a restored villa among the pine woods on the Princes' Island of Heybeli. *45 rooms | Refah Şehitleri Cad. 88 | Heybeliada | tel. 0216 3 51 00 25 | www.halki palacehotel.com*

LUXURY HOTELS

Çırağan Palace Kempinski (131 D4) (*m 0*)

Guests of state often rest their heads here, where a former sultan's palace was combined with a new hotel wing to make a truly delightful complex. In the warm season the outdoor bar right on the Bosphorus, the ● *Summer Lounge, is open. 316 rooms, 16 suites | from £ 250 | Çırağan Cad. 32 | Beşiktaş | tel. 0212 2 58 33 77 | www.kempinski.com/ istanbul*

Four Seasons ☆ (129 E5) (*m J7*)

Once a prison below Hagia Sophia, now stylishly restored and furnished to meet the very highest standards. Guests are treated to views across the historic quarter and the Sea of Marmara. *54 rooms, 11 suites | from £ 270 | Tevkifhane Sok. 1 | Sultanahmet | tel. 0212 6 38 82 00 | www.fourseasons.com/istanbul*

Four Seasons at the Bosphorus ☆ (131 D4) (*m 0*)

The Four Seasons was opened in 2009 in a restored Ottoman palace dating back to the 19th century with wonderful gardens and an outdoor pool right

by the sea. *166 rooms | from £ 330 | Çırağan Cad. 28 | Beşiktaş | tel. 0212 3 81 40 00 | www.fourseasons.com/ bosphorus*

Les Ottomans (131 D4) (*m 0*)

An old mansion that has been transformed into an Ottoman dream with a sumptuous spa. *10 suites | from £ 680 | Muallim Naci Cad. 68 | Kuruçeşme | tel. 0212 3 59 15 00 | www.lesottomans.com*

Pera Palace ⭐ (124 B3) (*m H3*)

The Pera Palace is the luxury hotel in the city! Built for passengers travelling on the Orient Express, patronised by writers and statesmen, it has now been returned to its former splendour. *150 rooms | from £ 250 | Meşrutiyet Cad. 52 | Tepebaşı (Beyoğlu) | tel. 0212 3 77 40 00 | www.perapalace.com*

Swissôtel The Bosphorus (131 D4) (*m L1*)

A modern luxury complex with every amenity above the sultan's palace. *600 rooms | from £ 220 | Bayıldım Cad. 2 | Maçka | tel. 0212 3 26 11 00 | www. swissotel.com*

A dream from the world of the Arabian Nights: Hotel Kybele

RAMADA ISTANBUL OLD CITY
(127 D4) *(🗺 C6)*

This comfortable hotel has a convenient location between the airport and the principal sights. It also boasts the excellent *Marmara* restaurant, a place to drink in *The North Shield Pub* and spa facilities. *100 rooms | Millet Cad. 82 | Fındıkzade (old quarter) | tel. 0212 6 31 20 20 | www.ramadaistanbul.com*

SPLENDID PALACE **(0)** *(🗺 0)*

A historic wooden building on the Princes' Island of Büyükada, and a splendid opportunity to get away from the hustle and bustle of İstanbul's city life. The hotel has a bright inner courtyard and an attractive outdoor pool. *70 rooms, 4 suites | Nisan Cad. 53 | Büyükada | tel. 0216 3 82 69 50 | www.splendidhotel.net*

SULTANAHMET PALACE
(129 E5) *(🗺 J7)*

This boutique hotel with a garden lies close to the Byzantine Mosaic Museum.

Each bathroom is like a little hamam, and there are ☼ INSIDER TIP de-luxe rooms with a view of the Blue Mosque or the Sea of Marmara. *36 rooms | Torun Sok. 19 | Sultanahmet | tel. 0212 4 58 04 60 | www.sultanahmetpalace.com*

TAXIM HILL ☼ **(125 D2)** *(🗺 K2)*

A good, comfortable and by all means recommendable city hotel in the heart of Pera. When you book, don't forget to ask for a room with a view of the Bosphorus! *50 rooms | Sıraselviler Cad. 5 | Taksim | tel. 0212 3 34 85 00 | www.taximhill.com*

HOTELS: BUDGET

BALE **(124 B3)** *(🗺 H3)*

The location of this hotel is convenient for getting around the city, but a bit noisy. Modern furnishings. ☼ Some rooms have a fine view of the Golden Horn. *63 rooms | Refik Saydam Cad. 55 | Tepebaşı-Beyoğlu | tel. 0212 2 53 07 00 | www.hotel-board.com*

BÜYÜK LONDRA (124 B3) (*H3*)

Come here to enjoy the charm of by-gone times: the *Grand Hotel de Londres*, known from Fatih Akin's film Crossing the Bridge, stands high above the Golden Horn in a central location. The interior is somewhat old-fashioned. Cheap rooms are to be had in the unrenovated wing. *54 rooms, 12 suites | Mesrutiyet Cad. 117 | Tepebaşı-Beyoğlu | tel. 0212 2 93 16 19 | www.londrahotel.net*

CİHANGİR HOTEL (125 D3) (*K2*)

Located in a quiet side street below Taksim Square behind the German Hospital (*Alman Hastanesi*), this hotel is a good address if you like the nightlife of the city . *35 rooms | Aslan Yatağı Sok. 33 | Cihangir-Beyoğlu | tel. 0212 2 51 53 17 | www.cihangirhotel.com*

GALATA ANTIQUE (124 B4) (*H3*)

At the end of the imposing historic İstiklal Caddesi boulevard, with decent rooms and a nice friendly atmosphere. *23 rooms | Mesrutiyet Cad. 119 | Tünel-Beyoğlu | tel. 0212 2 45 59 44 | www. galataantiquehotel.com*

MINA HOTEL ★ (129 D4) (*H7*)

Centrally situated city hotel with one of the most beautiful terrace restaurants in Sultanahmet and excellent value for money. *44 rooms | Piyerloti Cad., Dostluk Yurdu Sok. 6 | Cağaloğlu | tel. 0212 4 58 28 00 | www.minahotel.com.tr*

INSIDER TIP NAZ WOODEN HOUSE INN (129 E6) (*J8*)

A small hotel in Sultanahmet in a renovated old building that was constructed alongside the historic city wall. Modest-looking but a good choice! Pick-ups from the airport can be arranged. *7 rooms | Akbıyık Değirmeni Sok. 7 | Sultanahmet | tel. 0212 5 16 71 30 | www.nazwoodenhouseinn.com*

INSIDER TIP STONE HOTEL (129 E5) (*H7*)

Right in the middle of the old quarter, this historic building has impressive vaulted cellars, a garden and a nice terrace for sitting outdoors. *25 rooms | Binbirdirek Mah. Şehit Mehmet Paşa Yok. 34 | Sultanahmet | tel. 0212 6 38 15 54 | www.stonehotelistanbul.com*

A survivor from times past: the Büyük Londra is a strange but sublime place

UYAN ✂ (129 E5) (*⊘ J7*)

80-year-old restored wooden building at the heart of the tourist quarter with clean, simply furnished rooms. High up on the terrace, you can watch the light show that is staged every evening at the Blue Mosque. *26 rooms | Utangaç Sok. 25 | Sultanahmet | tel. 0212 5 16 48 92 | www.uyanhotel.com*

APARTMENTS

GALATA RESIDENCE (124 B5) (*⊘ H4*)

The building once belonged to the Camondo family, Jewish bankers who were prominent in high society life in Pera during İstanbul's belle époque. Today the house is divided into 15 apartments, all of them furnished in classical style. This is exactly the right place for those who love the charm of old Pera. *15 apartments | Galata, Bankalar Cad. Felek Sok. 2 | Karaköy | tel. 0212 2 92 48 41 | www.galataresidence.com | Moderate*

THE HOUSE APART (124 C3) (*⊘ J3*)

The apartments of the İstanbul coffeehouse chain The House are to be found on the European side of the city in Tünel, Galatasaray, Cihangir and Nişantaşı. These one- or two-room flats suitable for two people are comfortably furnished, and some of them have room for an additional bed. If desired room service and meals can be provided. *30 apartments | office: Firuzağa Mah. Bostanbaşı Cad. 19 | Beyoğlu | tel. 0212 2 49 87 34, mobile tel. 0533 6 03 86 48 | www.thehouseapart. com | Moderate*

HOSTELS

ORIENT HOSTEL (129 E5) (*⊘ J7*)

A clean, centrally located and comfortable hostel. There are some 'de-luxe' rooms with en-suite bathroom and a roof terrace. *40 rooms, 92 beds | Yeni Akbıyık Cad. 13 | Sultanahmet | tel. 0212 5 18 07 89 | www.orienthostel.com | Budget*

SINBAD HOSTEL ✂ (129 E5–6) (*⊘ H7*)

The options range from a bed in a six-bunk dorm (£ 7) to an en-suite double (£ 35). This is a quiet hostel with an attractive roof terrace. *22 rooms, 70 beds | Küçük Ayasofya Mah., Demirci Reşit Sok. 3/5 | Sultanahmet | tel. 0212 6 38 27 21 | www.sinbadhostel.com | Budget*

WORLD HOUSE HOSTEL (124 B4) (*⊘ H3*)

In a historic building and ideally situated: in the middle of the trendy district around the Galata Tower. There are beds in dormitories for £ 10 and comfortable double rooms for a little over £ 40. *Galip Dede Cad. 85 | Tünel-Beyoğlu | tel. 0212 2 93 55 20 | www.worldhouseistanbul. com | Budget*

LOW BUDGET

▶ For cheap but centrally located accommodation, try *Cordial House* **(129 D4)** (*⊘ H7*), a well-run hotel with everything you really need. Double rooms from £ 30. *40 rooms | Divanyolu Cad. Peykane Sok. 19 | Çemberlitaş | tel. 0212 5 18 05 76 | www.cordialhouse.com*

▶ The *Şen Palas* **(124 B3)** (*⊘ H3*) is definitely not a palace, but fairly basic accommodation at the heart of the Tünel entertainment quarter. Doubles £ 35. *25 rooms | Asmalı Mescit Sok. 30 | Beyoğlu | tel. 0212 2 93 84 37 | www.hotelsenpalas.com*

WALKING TOURS

The tours are marked in green in the street atlas,
the pull-out map and on the back cover

1 INSIGHTS INTO CHRISTIAN AND JEWISH İSTANBUL

İstanbul's old districts of Fener and Balat on the Golden Horn were the Christian and Jewish quarters in the Ottoman period. On this tour you can see impressive testimonies to the Christian culture of old Constantinople. Lasting approx. 5 to 6 hours, the walk takes you through one of the most interesting historic areas of İstanbul.

Start on the shore of the Golden Horn at Fener Vapur İskelesi, the ferry quay in Fener, reached by hourly ferries from Eminönü. From the quay – you will see a conspicuous police station there – enter the quarter and turn to Sadrazam

Ali Paşa Caddesi on your left. Here on the right behind high walls is the Greek Orthodox Patriarchate, where the head of the entire Orthodox church has lived since 1601. Although the Orthodox 'pope' does not have the same authority in the churches of Greece, Bulgaria, Serbia and Russia as the pope in Rome has for Roman Catholics, nevertheless they all recognise the patriarch of Constantinople as their spiritual leader. The building gained its present appearance in the course of a thorough restoration in the 18th century. Broad steps lead up to a large gateway with three doors, which is closed, as it has been since 1821 when the patriarch of the time, Grigorios V, supported the revolt against Turkish rule in what is now Greece and was

Photo: Gateway to the university in Beyazıt

An old Christian and Jewish quarter, and classical Ottoman mosques – walks in İstanbul are travels in time

hanged here for doing so. However, a gate at the side is now open to visitors, and you can at least take a look at the impressive ● **Patriarchate Church**. After that walk a few paces back to Yıldırım Caddesi and from there take a left into Vodina Caddesi, the main street of Fener. The rich Greeks of this quarter controlled trade in the Balkans and acted as translators and diplomats at the Ottoman court. From Vodina Caddesi turn left into Fener Kireçhanesi Sokak, which leads up to the **Boys' School**. This enor-

mous brick building rising majestically above Fener was once the main place of education for the İstanbul Greeks. Today it no longer has many pupils.

Behind the school turn right and walk around the whole complex to the **Mesnevihane Foundation** in the courtyard of a small mosque. On the right-hand side of the school, where your path heads downwards again, you first of all pass the modest-looking **Greek Girls' School** and then, on the left, reach the ancient Byzantine

INSIDER TIP Church of the Virgin Mary of the Mongols, a survivor from the time when the city was still called Constantinople. To see the interior of the church, ring the bell at the gate to call the verger, and you will be allowed inside in return for a small donation. A few yards further on you come to Çimen Sokak, which leads downhill back to Vodina Caddesi. Now bear right: on the left-hand side you will see some Greek townhouses, once magnificent but today in an extremely shabby state. As soon as you see an alley on the left leading down to the waterfront, go down to the road along the waterfront to see a restored Byzantine building that was once part of the city wall and today harbours something unique in the whole of Turkey, a INSIDER TIP women's library (Kadın Kütüphanesi) that was set up on the initiative of a feminist group. Only 200 metres further along the waterfront road stands the iron-built St Stephen's Church, the components of which were cast in 1871 in Vienna and shipped to İstanbul down the Danube and across the Black Sea. According to a legend the sultan permitted construction of the church on the condition that this took no more than a month. What is true is that the sultan feared the rise of nationalism among his Bulgarian subjects.

Beyond the church turn left again. Soon you will reach Balat, today a poor district of İstanbul and in a decayed condition. The second street parallel to the waterfront road is Vodina Caddesi again. Follow it as far as Ayan Sokak, and turn right there. In this street you will encounter the following sequence of buildings: an old hamam that is said to date back to the time of Mehmet the Conqueror, a beautiful mosque built by Sinan, the Feruh Kethüda Camii, and next to it the oldest Armenian church in the city, the Surp Hiresdagabad Church, which was originally a Byzantine building. In the late 15th century Jews who had been expelled from Spain settled in Balat – and on some houses the star of David can still be made out above the bay window. Many of the Jews who lived here emigrated to Israel in the 1950s, but others remain scattered around the city.

On the left Dürriye Sokak takes you to Gevgili Sokak, the site of İstanbul's oldest synagogue, the Ahrida (not open to the public). From here return to Kürkçü Çeşme Sokak, the shopping street serving this quarter, which leads uphill. Halfway up turn right into Pastırmacı Sokak, which consists of steps leading steeply up to Paşa Hamamı Sokak, where it ends. When you get to the top, on the right you will see a lovely ☕ tea garden with a view of the Golden Horn and the surrounding district. Now head left and walk for just over half a mile to the place where Kariye Türbe Camii Sokak turns off. Curving to the left, this lane will lead you straight to Chora Church → p. 38, which has the finest Byzantine mosaics in İstanbul.

From the Chora Church continue up Kariye Caddesi to the 1600-year-old city wall. It is wise to be on your guard in this poor district. A few hundred metres further on the right stands the Tekfur Sarayı, part of the old fortifications and the best-preserved part of the old Byzantine imperial palace. Under Ottoman rule it first served as a home for elephants and giraffes, and later as a secret brothel. Finally, the sultans used it as a new production site for the famous İznik tiles.

2 A CLASSIC WALK IN THE OLD QUARTER

This walk takes you across the historic peninsula from the Golden Horn almost to the Sea of Marmara. You will explore the old Muslim İstanbul beyond the Blue Mosque and the Topkapı Palace. This three to four-hour tour commences and closes with two important monuments from

and the interior are decorated with the famous İznik faiences, which cover large surfaces.

From the mosque follow the market lane until you come to the **Egyptian Bazaar** → p. 38. This historic market hall houses the city's spice bazaar. Here, in contrast to the situation in supermarkets, you can smell and taste the goods. Leave the spice bazaar heading in the direction of the old quarter and climb up the hill at a

İznik fayence adorns the interior of the impressive Rüstem Pasha Mosque

the classic phase of the Ottoman Empire: the Rüstem Pasha Mosque and the Sokullu Mehmet Pasha Mosque.

The **Rüstem Pasha Mosque (Rüstem Paşa Camii)** is situated a little inland from the road along the Golden Horn. It lies at the end of the **Tahtakale Market** → p. 41 and can be reached by walking up some steps from the road. It is one of the best examples of the work of the Ottoman architect Mimar Sinan and was built between 1561 and 1563 for Grand Vizier Rüstem Pasha. Both the façade

leisurely pace through the maze of alleyways. You will pass a lot of stores selling gold, clothing and items of everyday use. Many of these little shops are also wholesalers that supply clothes or jewellery to Anatolia. While strolling here don't overlook the centuries-old **caravanserais** with their beautiful courtyards. They are often hidden away and are used today for all kinds of purposes that have nothing to do with their origins as inns serving travellers. On Çakmakçılar Yokuşu continue walking uphill until you hit

Yaglikcilar Caddesi, which will lead you straight to the **Grand Bazaar → p. 40**. As a visit to this market offers enough diverting sights to keep anyone happy for several hours, if you wish to complete this tour it's better to make do with a quick glance inside the maze of shops.

At the end of Yağlıkçılar Caddesi, just before you meet the main road of Yeniçeriler Caddesi, keep an eye open on the right for the **Old Book Bazaar → p. 74**, which is well worth a look. Here you can buy everything from a valuable Koran to a second-hand thriller in English. The books are displayed on open market stalls in the way you might expect oranges to be sold. In the shops behind them, connoisseurs again and again happen on treasures for bibliophiles that you would hardly imagine at first glance. After passing through the book bazaar you reach a large square on which the main entrance of the venerable **university** is situated. The big gate is usually closed to visitors, however, as only the staff of the university and students are allowed inside. Opposite in the **Beyazıt Mosque (Beyazıt Camii)** this is not the case: visitors are most welcome. However, as with all Islamic places of worship, you should take into account the times for prayers. The mosque, one of the oldest in this part of İstanbul, is dedicated to Sultan Beyazıt II, the son of the conqueror of Constantinople. It was built in 1501 and is the first example of classical Ottoman mosque architecture, a style that was perfected decades later by Mimar Sinan.

Follow the main road to the left towards the Blue Mosque. A few hundred metres along on the left-hand side of the road you'll come across the **Çorlulu Ali Pasha Mosque (Çorlulu Ali Paşa Camii)**. This complex of buildings, one of the finest examples of the classical Ottoman style, was constructed in 1709. It includes a

The original classical Ottoman mosque: Beyazıt Mosque

house of prayer, premises for a sect, a religious college, a library and a small cemetery. The fountain facing the street was added after the great earthquake of 23 May 1766. Enter the courtyard to see the tea garden Çorlulu Ali Paşa Medresesi → p. 62. It is the oldest and probably the most charming meeting place for aficionados of the hookah (water pipe, or *nargile* in Turkish). If you would like to try out this traditional way of smoking, you will be in good company here: respectable elderly gentlemen inhale silently while they reminisce about the past.

Just a few paces further on, also on the left-hand side of the street, you pass the Column of Constantine → p. 41, one of the last remaining monuments from the early history of Constantinople. After that turn right into Klodfarer Caddesi and walk across Terzihane Sokak towards the ancient Hippodrome → p. 34. The Hippodrome was the centre of the city in the period of the Byzantine Empire. In the age of the Eastern Roman Empire the imperial box stood on the site today occupied by the Blue Mosque, and behind it was the imperial palace. Of the latter only the floors remain, and they can be admired in the Mosaic Museum → p. 34. The Hippodrome is also the location of the Museum of Islamic Art (Türk ve Islam Eserleri Müzesi). The imposing building that houses it was originally built for Grand Vizier Ibrahim Pasha and was later used as a barracks, storehouse and prison. In the 1980s the palace was restored and the museum moved into its spacious rooms, which are grouped around four courtyards. The collections of carpets, calligraphy and ceramics, as well as the ethnographic department with exhibits from all parts of Anatolia, make a visit extremely worthwhile. At the end of the Hippodrome take the road Şehit Mehmet Paşa Sokaği to the

Little remains of the Byzantine Hippodrome

last stop on this tour, the Sokullu Mehmet Pasha Mosque (Sokullu Mehmet Paşa Camii). Like the Rüstem Pasha Mosque it was built by Mimar Sinan to the commission of a grand vizier – exactly ten years later. The Sokullu Mehmet Pasha Mosque looks out onto the Sea of Marmara and like its sister is a masterpiece by court architect Sinan. Because the architect had more creative freedom here than in his designs for the great sultan's mosques, these two buildings are among the most impressive testimonies to the age of classical Ottoman architecture.

TRAVEL WITH KIDS

AĞVA (0) (*Đ 0*)

For stressed-out parents and frustrated kids the holiday resort of Ağva and its wonderful family bungalows lined up along the river Göksu are ideal. This is a great place for fishing, going for a walk, eating, swimming and paddling a boat. You can take a canoe to the mouth of the river at the Black Sea and have a good time fossicking for flotsam and jetsam, such as enormous fish bones. The *Riverside Club* with its pool is highly recommended. *Yakuplu Mahallesi 142 | Ağva | tel. 0216 7217136 | www.riverside.com.tr | Moderate*

ICE CREAM

İstanbul's ice-cream parlours are a delicious alternative to the products of well-known brands that come from the supermarket freezer. The quality of the ice cream isn't good everywhere, but you can't go wrong in the parlours of the Mado chain. *Daily 9am–10pm | İstiklal Cad. 188 (124 C2) (ĐĐ J2); Cumhuriyet Cad. 12 (125 D1) (ĐĐ K1); Elmadağ (Beyoğlu) | Selmanipak Cad. 1/A | Üsküdar (131 D5) (ĐĐ 0) | www.mado.com.tr.* İstanbul residents like to head for the promontory of Moda on the Asian side, where they not only get good ice cream

but also have lots of attractive tea gardens with a view across to the Topkapı Palace. *Daily 10am–midnight | Ali Usta, Moda Cad. 26 | Moda (131 D5) (ĐĐ 0)*

DONKEY RIDE ON BÜYÜKADA (0) (*ĐĐ 0*)

The Princes' Islands make a perfect day trip for families with children, and you can even spend your whole holiday in İstanbul on them. However, even just as an excursion they have lots to offer: INSIDER TIP take a ferry over in the morning, rent bikes by the quay and spend the whole day cycling round the island. Children can play under the great pine trees or ride a donkey in the Lunapark *(approx. £ 7)*. You can reach Büyükada by sea-bus, ferry or motorboat from Kabataş, Kadıköy or Bostancı. *Ticket £ 1–3 | departures from: island quay Adalar Iskelesi | up-to-date timetable: www.ido.com.tr.*

MINIATURK (130 C4) (*ĐĐ 0*)

On an area of round about 3.5 acres you and your children can admire models of famous buildings in Turkey and the whole Islamic world on the Golden Horn. A total of 120 models have been created to a scale of 1:25, enabling you to see the

The people of İstanbul are fantastic with children. Add the beach, miniature railway and donkey rides for a holiday full of fun!

Blue Mosque and other sights close up and from a completely new perspective, or to walk around on a miniature replica of the Bosphorus bridge. There is a large café serving snacks and drinks. *Daily 9am–6pm | admission approx. £ 3.50 | Sütlüce Mah., Imrahor Cad. | Sütlüce (at the end of the Golden Horn) | www.minia turk.com.tr*

INSIDER TIP **MOHINI** (131 D4) *(ʂ 0)*
This multi-storey children's paradise in Etiler above Bebek on the Bosphorus houses a Disney Corner and the Ikea Kids' Room amongst other attractions, as well as art studios, halls for gymnastics and an array of shops and restaurants for children. *Taxi from Beşiktaş | Tanburi Ali Efendi Sok. 15 | Etiler*

INSIDER TIP **RAHMI-KOÇ INDUSTRIAL MUSEUM** (123 D1–2) *(ʂ 0)*
This museum, donated by the industrial magnate Rahmi Koç, turns discovering technology into a real experience. Find out all about travel by rail, plane and ship and learn about developments in the fields of communications technology and astronomy. You can walk onto a captain's bridge, see a moored submarine and have fun with a miniature railway. *Tue–Sun 10am–5pm | admission approx. £ 4.50 | Hasköy Cad. 27 | Hasköy | www.rmk.museum.org.tr*

BEACHES FOR SWIMMING

The most popular places for cooling down or splashing around in the water are the Princes' Islands and the Black Sea in the north of the city. You can swim on the sandy beaches of *Kilyos* (131 D1) *(ʂ 0)*. A particularly attractive destination is the *Solar Beach Club. Access by municipal bus no. 151 from Sariyer | Turban Yolu Caddesi 4 | Kilyos | tel. 0212 2 01 21 39 | www.solar beach.net.* The beach of *Fenerbahçe Plaji* (131 D5) *(ʂ 0)* lies on the Asian side. It has wonderful loungers and a lovely pool! *Daily | admission approx. £ 10 | access by bus or taxi from Kadıköy*

FESTIVALS & EVENTS

From classical concerts in centuries-old churches to world stars performing under a starry sky, İstanbul stages one event after another, and they deservedly attracts crowds, especially in summer. Get advance information about the festivals in İstanbul at *www.istfest.org*, and tickets (which are reliably available for collection on the evening) at *www.biletix.com*.

PUBLIC HOLIDAYS

1 Jan *Yılbaşı*/New Year; **23 April** *Ulusal Egemenlik ve Çocuk Bayramı*/festival of national sovereignty and children; **1 May** *İşçi Bayramı*/Workers' Day; **19 May** *Gençlik ve Spor Bayramı*/festival of youth and sport; **30 Aug** *Zafer Bayramı*/celebration of victory in the wars of independence in 1922; **29 Oct** *Cumhuriyet Bayramı*/foundation day of the Turkish republic in 1923. **Religious holidays:** according to the lunar Islamic calendar religious festivals are held eleven days earlier each year: **20 July 2012/9 July 2013** start of Ramadan (month of fasting); **19–21 Aug 2012/8–10 Aug 2013** *Şeker Bayramı*/sugar festival, three-day conclusion to Ramadan; **25–28 Oct 2012/15–18 Oct 2013** *Kurban Bayramı*/ feast of sacrifice, the highest Islamic festival

EVENTS

▶ ★ *Dance of the dervishes* of the Mevlana Order: on Sundays at 3pm (in summer 5pm) and every second and last Saturday of the month at 3pm in the old house of the order, Galata Mevlevihanesi in Beyoğlu. *www.mekder.org*

MARCH/APRIL

▶ *International Film Festival:* the films are screened in selected cinemas in Beyoğlu and Kadıköy – all with subtitles. *www.film.iksv.org*
The ▶ *Tulip Festival* turns Emirgan Park into a sea of colour by the Bosphorus.

MAY

▶ *Theatre Biennial:* classical theatre, dance and street theatre with performers from Turkey and abroad; 2012, 2014, etc. *www.istfest.org/tiyatro*
▶ *Hidrellez:* on 5 and 6 May each year the Hidrellez spring festival is held at the Galata Tower and below Sultanahmet. It is a reminiscence of ancient pagan practices: Roma bands make music and people dance in the streets until the early hours. *www.hidrellez.org*

Whirling dervishes, international cinema and stars of the classical music scene – there are cultural highlights all year round

JUNE/JULY

▶ ● **International Music Festival:** music, dance and opera; the highlight is a performance of Mozart's Il Seraglio. Open-air stages and the Byzantine Aya Irini Church in the garden of the Topkapı Palace are the venues for musical treats.

▶ INSIDER TIP **International Jazz Festival:** major international artists of the genre perform in concert halls, on the streets and in jazz clubs. *www.iksv.org*

▶ **Rock'n Coke:** every July Hezarfen Airport is transformed into a giant open-air stage for two days. 10,000 music-lovers pitch their tents all over the airfield to see acts by international and Turkish musicians. *www.rockncoke.com or www. biletix.com*

AUGUST

On 15/16 Aug the traditional ▶ **Yelken Yarışları** sailing regatta is held. In late summer offshore races take place in Bebek. *www.tyf.org.tr*

The ▶ **Akbank Festival of Short Films** at-tracts mainly young filmmakers from all over southern Europe and the Caucasus.

SEPTEMBER

Since 2003 artists have organised the ▶ **Tünel Art Festival** around Galata Tower. From late September to mid-October the ▶ **Akbank Jazz Festival** livens things up on the streets and ferries.

OCTOBER

The ▶ **Efes Pilsen Blues Festival** draws some of the big names in American blues to the Bosphorus. Various venues. *www. efesblues.com.*

NOVEMBER

Since 1987 the ▶ **İstanbul Biennial** has been pulling in Turkish and international artists (2013, 2015, etc.). *www.iksv.org*

DECEMBER

The main Christmas Mass is celebrated in ▶ **St Anthony's Church** on İstiklal Caddesi (24 Dec, 9pm).

LINKS, BLOGS, APPS & MORE

LINKS

▶ http://english.istanbul.com/ This website is a useful guide to the city, offering you tips on shopping, entertainment and accommodation as well as a calendar of events and a photo gallery to help you decide where to go

▶ www.biletix.com.tr Click on the English version of this site to get information on cultural events and sports, and to order tickets online which can either be sent to your hotel by courier or picked up at the box office on the night

▶ www.turkishculture.org A well-produced survey of Turkish culture with explanations and good photos: architecture, music, food and many arts and crafts such as ceramics and carpets

▶ http://harita.iett.gov.tr/en The English-language version of the official portal of the municipal transport authority. An interactive map helps you find the right bus for your destination

▶ www.istfest.org Website of the İstanbul foundation for art and culture, which organises the film, theatre, music and jazz festivals as well as the art biennial

▶ www.kultur.gov.tr Here the Turkish Ministry of Tourism and Culture presents comprehensive information in English about the city and its sights, as well as background information on the country and details of sightseeing in other cities and regions

▶ www.booksfromturkey.com The Ministry of Tourism and Culture's English-language presentation of books on all kinds of subjects

APPS

▶ Global GPS Audio Travel Guide This app for iPhone provides you with GPS and mapping information as well as an audioguide to the principal sights

▶ Istanbul Sights iPhone app with an easy-to-use map of İstanbul marking the relevant destinations

Regardless of whether you are still preparing your trip or already in İstanbul: these addresses will provide you with more information, videos and networks to make your holiday even more enjoyable

▶ Spotted by locals Bang-up-to-date reports by four city residents, now available as an app, a spin-off from the superb www.spottedbylocals.com site

▶ www.iwasinturkey.com/photos Lots and lots of pics, and links to even more on flickr

▶ www.istanbultrails.com The video gallery on this site gives you a taster of a Bosphorus cruise and many of the main sights; the articles take a refreshingly critical approach to tourism in İstanbul

▶ www.tourvideos.com Click on Turkey/İstanbul for videos showing you the Grand Bazaar, Blue Mosque and much more

▶ www.britishcouncil.org/turkey.htm Information about the activities of the British Council in İstanbul, including various social and cultural projects. There is a blog, as well as links to Twitter and Facebook pages

▶ www.mymerhaba.com This site has an events calendar and lots of tips for foreigners living in Turkey, including a variety of forums where contributors exchange news about practical matters and provide entertainment tips

▶ www.istanbulbuddy.co.uk Packed with information about sightseeing, going out, and eating, with links to blogs

▶ www.squidoo.com/living_Istanbul A personal view by a native of the city about what's wonderful... and what's frustrating

▶ http://locallypera.blogspot.com/ Lots of tips about shopping and eating in the Pera district, by an insider

▶ www.facebook.com/pages/TOPHANE-ART-WALK/107770535911925 The Tophane Art Walk is a cooperative venture by small independent art galleries in the Tophane district. This Facebook page gives you up-to-date information on the scene

▶ www.facebook.com/istanbulmodernsanatmuzesi İstanbul Modern puts details of forthcoming events on its Facebook page

TRAVEL TIPS

ARRIVAL

✈ The airport in İstanbul at which scheduled flights and almost all charter flights land is Atatürk Hava Limanı in Yeşilköy *(www.dhmiata.gov.tr)*. Some of the budget airlines (e.g. Easyjet) now also use Sabiha Gökçen Airport on the Asian side *(www.sgairport.com)*. British Airways and Turkish Airways fly to İstanbul from London, Easyjet from Luton. If you find no convenient cheap direct link from the UK, a flight via a European hub is worth considering. Germanwings and Air Berlin, for example, fly from UK airports to Berlin and from there to İstanbul. Turkish Airlines fly from New York to İstanbul. From other North American destinations, the options are various European and US carriers with connections via New York or Europe. There are round-the-clock shuttle buses from both airports to the city centre, and a rail service links Atatürk Airport with Kabataş or Eminönü/Sultanahmet, though you have to change in Aksaray.

A taxi to Sultanahmet from Yeşilköy costs about £ 12, from Sabiha-Gökçen at least £ 25. Night journeys cost 50 per cent more.

🚗 To drive to Turkey from London you have to cross France, Germany, the Czech Republic, Slovakia, Hungary, Serbia and Bulgaria, obviously not a relaxing way to get there and also unsafe, as the traffic is chaotic in places.

🚌 A cheap but tiring alternative is to get a budget flight to almost any German city and catch a coach taking Turkish residents of Germany to İstanbul.

🚃 The Balkan Express goes from Munich to İstanbul via Salzburg, Vienna, Budapest and Sofia, taking 40 hours (i.e. well over 50 hours from London) and costing more than a budget flight.

🚢 The romantic way to arrive is by ship from Venice or Brindisi, but the voyage will set you back £ 350 or more per car.

RESPONSIBLE TRAVEL

It doesn't take a lot to be environmentally friendly whilst travelling. Don't just think about your carbon footprint whilst flying to and from your holiday destination but also about how you can protect nature and culture abroad. As a tourist it is especially important to respect nature, look out for local products, cycle instead of driving, save water and much more. If you would like to find out more about eco-tourism please visit: *www.ecotourism.org*

BANKS & CHANGING MONEY

Banks are generally open from Monday to Friday from 8.30am till midday and from 1.30pm to 5pm. Many do not close at midday and also open on Saturdays *(öğlen açık)*. You can change money in exchange bureaus and in all banks. There are no problems in İstanbul about getting cash from an ATM/cashpoint with your bank card, and the usual credit cards are widely accepted.

CONSULATES

BRITISH CONSULATE
Mesrutiyet Caddesi no. 34 | Tepebasi Be-

From arrival to weather

Holiday from start to finish: useful addresses and information for your trip to İstanbul

yoglu 34435 | Istanbul | Turkey | tel. +90 212 334 6400 | fax +90 212 334 6401 | http://ukinturkey.fco.gov.uk/
US CONSULATE
İstinye Mahallesi | Üç Şehitler Sokak no. 2 | İstinye 34460 | Istanbul | Turkey | tel. +90 212 335 90 00 | http://istanbul.us-consulate.gov/

CURRENCY & PRICES

The Turkish currency is called *Türk Lirası* (TL). There are notes of 50, 20, 10 and 5 TL, and coins for 1 TL, 50 *kuruş*, 25, 10, 5 and 1 *kuruş*.

There are considerable differences in price levels between Turkey and western Europe, especially for clothes and shoes. Local products tend to be 30 to 60 per cent cheaper than foreign brands, and food is also cheaper in Turkey – at least from market stalls and supermarkets, not necessarily in a restaurant! Fruit and vegetables are very cheap in season; meat is more expensive owing to the military conflict with Kurdish separatists, as domestic production has fallen and most meat has to be imported from abroad. Precious stones and souvenirs usually seem good value to visitors from North American and Europe. Keep an eye on the prices for beer and wine in cafés, bars and restaurants – these alcoholic drinks are often overpriced, so don't fail to look at the menu!

CUSTOMS

There are no restrictions on the import of foreign or Turkish currency to Turkey. The duty-free allowance on arriving is 200 cigarettes or 20 cigars and 5 litres of alcoholic drinks. If you arrive by car, the vehicle is noted in your passport.

The export of ancient (i.e. more than 100-year-old) items is prohibited. To take other old items out of the country you need a permit from a museum director. Travellers returning to the European Union have the following duty-free allowance: 200 cigarettes, 250 g of tobacco or 50 cigars, 2 litres of wine and 1 litre of spirits, 500 g of coffee, 50 g of perfume, 250 ml of eau de toilette and other goods to a value of £ 390 (when flying); to the USA (see *www.cbp.gov* for all details) normally goods to a value of $ 800 including 2 litres of alcoholic drinks.

DRINKING WATER

Although the tap water is chlorinated, it is best to use it for cooking rather than drinking.

ELECTRICITY

The power supply in Turkey is 220-volt alternating current. Travellers from the UK, Ireland and North America need an adapter to fit the Turkish two-pin sockets.

EMERGENCY

Tourist police: tel. 5 27 45 03
National emergency no.: tel. 155
Medical emergency: tel. 0212 4 44 09 11 or 112
Emergency helicopter (International Hospital): tel. 0212 6 63 30 00

GETTING YOUR BEARINGS

The municipal area of İstanbul has multiple divisions. The Bosphorus separates the European *(Avrupa Yakası)* from the Asian side *(Asya)*. The administrative districts *(ilce)* are subdivided into quarters *(semt)* and these in turn into neighbourhoods *(mahalle)*. When you are looking for an address it is often useful to know the name of the neighbourhood too.

For the addresses in this guide, you will find details of the district, quarter or neighbourhood if this is helpful for finding your way. The division of the city in the Sightseeing chapter does not correspond to the official administrative boundaries but follows the principle of what interests visitors to İstanbul.

HEALTH

If you need a doctor, ask at your hotel or a tourist information office. Pharmacies *(eczane)* are well stocked. No vaccinations are needed before travelling.

INTERNATIONAL HOSPITAL
Yeşilyurt | İstanbul | tel. 0212 468 44 44 | www.internationalhospital.com.tr

AMERICAN HOSPITAL
Güzelbahçe Sokak | Nişantaşı, İstanbul | tel. 0212 311 2000 | www.amerikanhastanesi.com.tr

BUDGETING

Taxi	£ 0.50 / $ 0.80
	per kilometre
Coffee	£ 0.80 / $ 1.25
	for Turkish coffee
Ferry	£ 1.60 / $ 2.50
	across the Bosphorus
Wine	£ 3 / $ 4.70
	for a glass
Snack	£ 1.25 / $ 2
	for döner kebab
CD	Approx. £ 5 / $ 8
	for Turkish music

IMMIGRATION

British and other EU citizens need no visa, only a valid passport or identity card. The maximum length of stay is three months (EU citizens arriving with an identity card but no passport should keep the stamped immigration form). American citizens travelling to Turkey on U.S. passports must obtain a visa. Currently, holders of all types of passports can purchase a 90-day sticker visa at the port of entry for $ 20 cash if they are tourists.

INFORMATION BEFORE YOU TRAVEL

TURKISH TOURISM AND INFORMATION OFFICES
UK
29-30 St James's Street | London SW1A 1HB | United Kingdom | tel. 020 7839 77 78 or 7839 78 02 | www.gototurkey.co.uk

USA - New York
821 United Nations Plaza | New York N.Y. 10017 | USA | tel. 1 212 687 21 94 | e-mail: ny@tourismturkey.org, newyork@goturkey.com

INFORMATION IN İSTANBUL

ATATÜRK AIRPORT (ATATÜRK HAVA LIMANI)
(130 A6) *(ØØ 0)* *Yeşilköy (inside the terminal) | open 24 hours | tel. 0212 6 63 07 04 | www.dhmiata.gov.tr*

KARAKÖY
(124 B5) *(ØØ H4)* *Karaköy Yolcu Salonu (inside the terminal) | daily 7am–10pm | tel. 0212 2 49 57 76 | www.tdi.com.tr*

SULTANAHMET
(129 E5) *(ØØ H7)* *Sultanahmet Meydanı information pavilion (at the bus stop) | daily 9am–7pm | tel. 0212 5 18 18 02*

TAKSIM

(125 D1) (*K1*) *Hilton Oteli Girişi (at the hotel entrance) | daily 8am–7pm | tel. 0212 2 33 05 92*

NEWSPAPERS

Major English magazines and newspapers are generally available on the day of publication, American publications a day later. There are stands selling international press in Tünel, on Taksim Square, at Divan Yolu, in Kadıköy by the ferry quay and in larger hotels. There are also local publications in English: Turkish Daily News and New Anatolian, as well as the events and listings magazines Time Out (monthly) and İstanbul Guide (quarterly).

PERSONAL SAFETY

The embassies of the USA and UK provide detailed information to travellers on their websites http://ukinturkey.fco.gov.uk/ and *http://istanbul.usconsulate.gov/* about the security situation.

PHONE & MOBILE PHONE

Public phones are all card phones. You can use them for calls abroad. Buy phone cards *(telefon kartı)* from post offices or street vendors near the phone.

You can use mobile phones from Euro-

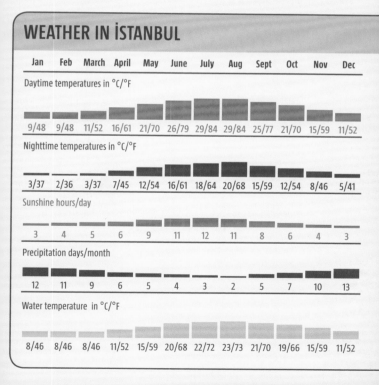

WEATHER IN İSTANBUL

	Jan	Feb	March	April	May	June	July	Aug	Sept	Oct	Nov	Dec
Daytime temperatures in °C/°F	9/48	9/48	11/52	16/61	21/70	26/79	29/84	29/84	25/77	21/70	15/59	11/52
Nighttime temperatures in °C/°F	3/37	2/36	3/37	7/45	12/54	16/61	18/64	20/68	15/59	12/54	8/46	5/41
Sunshine hours/day	3	4	5	6	9	11	12	11	8	6	4	3
Precipitation days/month	12	11	9	6	5	4	3	2	5	7	10	13
Water temperature in °C/°F	8/46	8/46	8/46	11/52	15/59	20/68	22/72	23/73	21/70	19/66	15/59	11/52

pean countries in Turkey *(information: www.gsmworld.com)*. Turkey has three networks: Turkcell, Vodafone and Aria. If you have a Turkish prepaid card, you pay no charges for incoming calls. Using your mailbox can be expensive, so switch if off before you leave home! Dialling codes:

UK: 0044
Ireland: 00353
USA/Canada: 001
Turkey: 0090
İstanbul, European side: 0090/212;
İstanbul, Asian side: 0090/216

If you make a trans-Bosphorus call within the city, use the code 0216 for Asia or 0212 for Europe.

POST

Post offices are marked with a yellow PTT sign. Letters and cards to the UK usually take a week, to North America almost certainly longer. *Opening times: Mon–Fri 8.30am–midday and 1pm–5pm*

PUBLIC TRANSPORT

In İstanbul the best means of transport alongside the trams and the cable cars between Karaköy-Tünel and Kabataş-Taksim is a taxi. It's good value for money, costing about a third less than in most western European countries. From midnight to 6am the night tariff operates, 50 per cent higher. But do take care when travelling by taxi: make sure before you set off that the driver knows the place you want to go, and check that the taximeter is switched on. The cheap and popular shared taxis (called *dolmuş, the*

BOOKS & FILMS

▶ **İstanbul. Memories of a City** – These autobiographical essays (2006) by Orhan Pamuk, winner of the Nobel Prize for Literature, provide a key to understanding the city

▶ **İstanbul. Poetry of Place** – An anthology of writings from different eras and cultures, from Sultan Süleyman to W B Yeats, edited by Ates Orga

▶ **Sweet Waters** – A tale of political intrigue and love during the last years of the Ottoman Empire by Harold Nicolson, who was a diplomat in the old İstanbul of those days, republished in 2000

▶ **Topkapi** – Famous 1964 İstanbul film starring Sir Peter Ustinov, Melina Mercouri and Robert Morley, based on a novel by Eric Ambler about a plot to steal the emerald-studded dagger of the sultans

▶ **James Bond** – Two Bond films are set partly in İstanbul. In 1963 the city supplied an atmospheric backdrop to Sean Connery in 'From Russia with Love'. In 1999 the Leander Tower in the Bosphorus gave Pierce Brosnan a thrilling end to 'The World is not Enough'

▶ **Crossing the Bridge** – This great act of cinematic homage to the city (2005) by Fatih Akin, born in Hamburg of Turkish descent, is a documentary about İstanbul's vibrant and extremely diverse music scene

Turkish word for 'filled') don't set off until they are – *yes, filled*. There are *dolmuş* on main squares such as Taksim.

Buses are normally overcrowded and move slowly due to congestions. If you still want to take one, you will find bus stations at Taksim, in Karaköy, Eminönü and on Hürriyet Meydanı in Beyazıt. On the Asian side, in Kadıköy and Üsküdar, buses run from the ferry quays. Tickets for those are sold at counters *(bilet)*, but usually you can pay the driver in cash. If you stay for more than a few days it's worthwhile buying an *akbil* (recharge-able electronic ticket).

The fast central tramline *(Hızlı Tramvay)* runs from Kabataş via Eminönü and Sultanahmet to Zeytinburnu. In Aksaray you change for Atatürk Airport *(daily 6am–midnight / approx. £ 0.50)*. Karaköy and İstiklal Caddesi (Beyoğlu) are linked by the *Tünel* cableway. From Kabataş you can also take a cable car *(finiculère)* up to Taksim Square. The Metro runs between Taksim Square and Maslak *(daily 6.15am–0.30am, every 5 minutes / 8 stops / approx. £ 0.70)*. The main piers for ferries and sea buses are Eminönü, Karaköy, Kabataş, Beşiktaş, Üsküdar and Kadıköy *(www.ido.com.tr)*. A rather crowded *Metrobus* operates on its own lane in Aksaray and Kadıköy.

As the best way to get round in İstanbul is a taxi, other means of transport are mentioned in this guide only where advantageous.

TIPPING

In cafés, bars and restaurants a tip of approx. 10 per cent is normal. In taxis you are not always expected to round up the fare, as tips for taxi drivers are not the norm: just take your change and get out. If you want to use any special service in a hotel (or some other establishment), offer a tip in advance or make it clear that you are willing to. This will help you get what you want.

A wonderful old example of the famous pool taxis

CURRENCY CONVERTER

£	TRY	TRY	£
1	2.78	1	0.36
3	8.35	3	1.08
5	13.90	5	1.78
13	36.20	13	4.67
40	111	40	14
75	208	75	27
120	334	120	43
250	695	250	90
500	1,390	500	180

$	TRY	TRY	$
1	1.77	1	0.56
3	5.32	3	1.70
5	8.88	5	2.82
13	23	13	7.30
40	71	40	22.50
75	133	75	42
120	213	120	68
250	444	250	140
500	888	500	280

For current exchange rates see www.xe.com

USEFUL PHRASES TURKISH

PRONUNCIATION

ı	like 'a' in 'ago', e.g.: ırmak
c	like 'j' in 'jump', e.g.: cam
ç	like 'ch' in 'chat', e.g.: çan
h	like English 'h', or 'ch' in Scottish 'loch', e.g.: hamam
ğ	a silent letter than extends the vowel before it, e.g.: yağmur
j	like 's' in 'leisure', e.g.: jilet
ş	like 'sh' in 'ship', e.g.: teker
v	like 'v' in 'violin', e.g.: vermek
y	like 'y' in 'young', e.g.: yok
z	like 'z' in 'zoom', e.g.: deniz

IN BRIEF

Yes/No/Maybe	Evet/Hayır/Belki
Please/Thank you	Lütfen/Teşekkür (ederim) or Mersi
Excuse me, please!	Afedersin/ Afedersiniz
May I ...?	İzin verir misiniz?
Pardon?	Efendim? Nasıl?
I would like to .../Have you got ...?	... istiyorum/... var mı?
How much is ...?	... ne kadar? Fiyatı ne?
I (don't) like that	Beğendim/Beğenmedim
good/bad	iyi/kötü
broken/doesn't work	bozuk/çalışmıyor
too much/much/little	çok fazla/çok/ az
all/nothing	hepsi/hiç
Help!/Attention!/Caution!	İmdat!/Dikkat!/Aman!
ambulance	ambulans
police/fire brigade	polis/itfaiye
Prohibition/forbidden	yasak/ yasak

GREETINGS, FAREWELL

Good morning!/afternoon!/ evening!/night!	Günaydın/İyi Günler!/ İyi Akşamlar!/İyi Geceler!
Hello! / Goodbye!	Merhaba!/Allaha ısmarladık!
See you	Hoşçakal (plural: Hoşçakalın)

Türkçe biliyormusun?

'Do you speak Turkish?' This guide will help you to say the basic words and phrases in Turkish.

DATE & TIME

Monday/Tuesday/Wednesday	Pazartesi/Salı/Çarşamba
Thursday/Friday/Saturday	Perşembe/Cuma/Cumartesi
Sunday/working day	Pazar/İş günü
Holiday	Tatil Günü/Bayram
today/tomorrow/yesterday	bugün/yarın/dün
hour/minute	saat/dakika
day/night/week	gün/gece/hafta
month/year	ay/yıl
What time is it?	Saat kaç?

TRAVEL

open/closed	açık/kapalı
departure/arrival	kalkış/varış
toilets / ladies/gentlemen	tuvalet (WC) / bayan/bay
Where is ...?/Where are ...?	Nerede ...?/ neredeler ...?
left/right	sol/sağ
straight ahead/back	ileri/geri
close/far	yakın/uzak
bus/tram/underground / taxi/cab	otobüs/tramvay/metro / taksi
bus stop/cab stand	durak/taksi durağı
parking lot/parking garage	park yeri/otopark
train station/harbour/airport	istasyon/liman/havaalanı
schedule/ticket	tarife/bilet
single/return	tek gidiş/gidiş dönüş
train/track	tren/peron
I would like to rent ...	... kiralamak istiyorum
a car	bir otomobil/araba
a boat/rowing boat	bir tekne/sandal
petrol/gas station	benzin istasyonu
petrol/gas / diesel	benzin/dizel
leaded/unleaded	kurşunlu/kurşunsuz
breakdown/repair shop	arıza/tamirhane

FOOD & DRINK

Could you please book a table for tonight for four?	Lütfen bize bu akşama dört kişilik bir masa ayırın.
on the terrace/by the window	terasta/pencere kenarında
The menu, please	menü lütfen

Could I please have ...?	... alabilir miyim lütfen?
bottle/carafe/glass	şişe/karaf/bardak
knife/fork/spoon	bıçak/çatal/kaşık
salt/pepper/sugar/vinegar/oil	tuz/karabiber/şeker/sirke/zeytinyağı
milk/cream/lemon	süt/kaymak/limon
cold/too salty/not cooked	soğuk/fazla tuzlu/pişmemiş
with/without ice	buzlu/buzsuz
Water sparkling/still	su/soda
vegetarian/allergy	vejetaryan/alerji
May I have the bill, lease?	Hesap lütfen
bill/receipt/tip	fatura/fiş/bahşiş

SHOPPING

Where can I find...?	... nerede bulurum?
I'd like .../I'm looking for ...	... istiyorum/... arıyorum
Do you put photos onto CD?	CD'ye fotoğraf basıyor musnuz?
pharmacy/chemist	eczane/parfümeri
baker/market	fırın/pazar
shopping centre/department store	alışveriş merkezi/bonmarşe
grocery/supermarket	gıda marketi, bakkal/süpermarket
100 grammes/1 kilo	yüz gram/bir kilo
expensive/cheap/price	pahalı/ucuz/fiyat
more/less	daha çok/daha az

ACCOMMODATION

I have booked a room	Bir oda rezervasyonum var
Do you have any ... left?	Daha ... var mı?
Single bed/single room	tek yataklı/tek kişilik oda
Double bed/double room	çift yataklı/çift kişilik oda
breakfast/half board/	kahvaltı/yarım pansiyon/
full board (American plan)	tam pansiyon
at the front/seafront	ön tarafta/denize bakan
shower/sit-down bath	duş/banyo
key/room card	anahtar/oda kartı
luggage/suitcase/bag	bagaj/bavul/çanta

BANKS, MONEY & CREDIT CARDS

bank/ATM	banka/ATM
pin code	şifre
I'd like to change ...	... bozduracağım
cash/credit card	nakit/kredi kartı
bill/coin	banknot/demir para
change	bozuk para

HEALTH

doctor/dentist/paediatrician	doktor/diş doktoru/çocuk doktoru
hospital/emergency clinic	hastane/acil doktor
fever/pain	ateş/ağrı
diarrhoea/nausea/sunburn	ishal/bulantı/güneş yanığı
inflamed/injured	iltihaplı/yaralı
plaster/bandage	yara bandı/gazlı bez
ointment/cream	merhem/krem
pain reliever/tablet	ağrı kesici/hap

POST, TELECOMMUNICATIONS & MEDIA

stamp/postcard/letter	posta pulu/kartpostal/mektup
I need a phone card	Bir telefon kartı lazım
I'm looking for a prepaid card	Bir hazırkart lazım
Where can I find internet access?	İnternete nereden girebilirim?
dial/connection/engaged	çevirmek/hat/meşgul
socket/adapter/charger	priz/adaptör/şarj aleti
computer/battery/rechargeable battery	bilgisayar/pil/akü
internet connection/wifi	internet bağlantısı/wireless
e-mail/file/print	(e-)mail (e-posta)/dosya/basmak

LEISURE, SPORTS & BEACH

beach/bathing beach	sahil/plaj
sunshade/lounger	(güneş) şemsiye(si)/şezlong
low tide/high tide/current	med/cezir/akıntı

NUMBERS

0	sıfır		15	on beş
1	bir		16	on altı
2	iki		17	on yedi
3	üç		18	on sekiz
4	dört		19	on dokuz
5	beş		20	yirmi
6	altı		21	yirmi bir
7	yedi		50	elli
8	sekiz		100	yüz
9	dokuz		200	iki yüz
10	on		1000	bin
11	onbir		2000	iki bin
12	oniki		10000	on bin
13	on üç		½	yarım
14	on dört		¼	çeyrek

NOTES

FOR YOUR NEXT HOLIDAY ...

MARCO POLO TRAVEL GUIDES

ALGARVE
AMSTERDAM
BARCELONA
BERLIN
BRUSSELS
BUDAPEST
CALIFORNIA
COLOGNE
CORFU
CRETE
DUBAI
DUBROVNIK &
  DALMATIAN
  COAST
EDINBURGH
EGYPT

FINLAND
FLORENCE
FLORIDA
FRENCH RIVIERA
  NICE, CANNES &
  MONACO
IRELAND
ISTANBUL
KOS
LAKE GARDA
LANZAROTE
LONDON

LOS ANGELES
MADEIRA
  PORTO SANTO
MALLORCA
MALTA
  GOZO
NEW YORK
NORWAY
PARIS
RHODES
ROME

SAN FRANCISCO
SICILY
SOUTH AFRICA
STOCKHOLM
THAILAND
TURKEY
  SOUTH COAST
VENICE

MARCO POLO
With ROAD ATLAS & PULL-OUT MAP
LAKE GARDA
MONTE BALDO WITH MOUNTAIN BIKE
The car in Malcesine takes bikes too
"KISSES" IN SALÒ
Chocolate "Baceti"
Travel with Insider Tips

MARCO POLO
With STREET ATLAS & PULL-OUT MAP
NEW YORK
MEADOWS, WILD FLOWERS AND SKYSCRAPERS
Green is chic: the High Line in Chelsea
COCKTAIL ON CLOUD NINE
Rooftop bar at 230 Fifth Street
Travel with Insider Tips

MARCO POLO
With ROAD ATLAS & PULL-OUT MAP
FRENCH RIVIERA
NICE, CANNES & MONACO
SPECTACULAR GRAND CANYON DU VERDON
Breath-taking scenery that takes some beating
SNIFFING THE AIR
The perfume manufacturers of Grasse
Travel with Insider Tips
www.marco-polo.com

MARCO POLO
With ROAD ATLAS & PULL-OUT MAP
MALLORCA
AN FLAIR IN THE MEDITERRANEAN
Mallorca's most beautiful beach
E ..."IN" CROWD MEET
...ronda in Deià
Travel with Insider Tips

MARCO POLO
With STREET ATLAS & PULL-OUT MAP
BERLIN
A STUNNING ISLAND JUST FOR ART
Showcasing treasures from around the world
STAY COOL AT NIGHT
...b scene sets the trend
Travel with Insider Tips

- PACKED WITH INSIDER TIPS
- BEST WALKS AND TOURS
- FULL-COLOUR PULL-OUT MAP
  AND STREET ATLAS

STREET ATLAS

The green line ▬▬ indicates the Walking tours (p. 96–101)

All tours are also marked on the pull-out map

Photo: Four Seasons Hotel

Exploring İstanbul

The map on the back cover shows how the area
has been sub-divided

This is a map of the Beyoğlu, Tepebaşı, Galata, and Karaköy areas of Istanbul.

Grid references (columns A, B, C; rows 1–6)

Pangaltıpaşa Bulvarı
Derya Beyi Sk.
Kankaralar Sk.
Hacı Hasan Sk.
Pilikçi
Kamer Hatun Sk.
Taksim
Şişhane Kuşdili

CUMH

Dolapdere Caddesi
Kadı Sk.
Büyük Yokuş Sk.
Pir Hüsamettin Sk.
Eburrıza Derg. Sk.
Dalles Teşrifatçı Oya Sk.
 Hortumcu Sk.
Kara Kurum Sk.

Ağaç Köprü Sk.
Kasımpaşa Aracısı Sk.
Dolapdere Caddesi
Ömer Hayyam Cad.

Pişmaniye
Bahriye Caddesi
Tepebaşı Vatan Hastanesi

BEYOĞLU

Tarlabaşı
Süslü Saksı Sk.
Ağa Camii
Kural
İstiklal Caddesi

Kızılay Meyd. Cad.
Hoca Ahmet Sk.
A. Emin Yalman Ortaokulu İlk.
Kasım Paşa Camii
Bedreddin Camii
Aşıklar Meydanı
TEPEBAŞI
Kamer Hatun Bulvarı
Arslan Sk.
Hamalbaşı Cad.
Çiçek Pasajı
Galatasaray
IRT Stüdyolare
St. Antuan Kilisesi
Galatasaray Lisesi
Galatasaray Hamamı
Çukurcuma Camii
Taksim
Ha

Turabi Baba Sk.
Bahriye Caddesi
Fatih Sk.
Haliç Kapısı
Havuz
Büyük Kasımpaşa Camii
Çivici Sk.
Recep T. Erdoğan Stadyumu
Tepebaşı Parkı
SALT
Pera Müzesi
Ziya Sk.
Fransız Sokağı
Firuzağa Camii
Hacıpiri Camii
Deftardar Yoku

zayirli Gazi Hasan Parkı
Eviliya Çelebi Caddesi
Anbar Arkası Sk.
Şişhane
TÜNEL
Asmalı Mescit Sk.
Tomtom Kaptan Camii
Tomtom Kaptan Sk.
Boğazkesen Cad.
İtalyan Hast.

ŞİŞHANE
Refik
Yolcuzade İskender Cad.
Beyoğlu Ticaret Lisesi
N. Hanım Sk.
Galip Dede Cad.
Tünel
Mevlevihane Müzesi
Santa Maria Kilisesi
Alman Lisesi
TOPHANE
Tophane Binası
Tophane

Azapkapı Çeşmesi
Okmeydanı Camii
Okçu Musa Caddesi
Hoca Ali Camii
Kılıç Ali Paşa Camii
Kılıç Ali Pş. Hamamı

Azapkapı Sokullu M. Paşa Camii
Tersane Cad.
Arap Camii
Galata Kulesi
Galata Yüksek Kaldırım
St. Benoit
GALATA
SALT
Kemeraltı Caddesi
Necatibey Cad.

rüsü
Bankalar Cad.
St. George Hast.
Karaköy
KARAKÖY
Denizcilik İşletmel. Müdürlüğü

5
Tersane Cad.
Kürekçiler Kapısı Sk.
Fermenciler Cad.
Yeraltı Camii
Karaköy Meyd.
Kemankeş Müst. Ps.
Deniz Otobüsü İskelesi

Eyup-Beyoğlu-Fatih-Eminönü-Üsküdar
Haliç
Karaköy Vapur İskelesi
Rıhtım Cad.

İstanbul Ticaret Odası
Galata Köprüsü

6
Sobacılar Cad.
Ahi Çelebi Camii
Çeşme Cad.
Demirtaş Mescidi
Rüstem Paş. Hamamı
129
Rüst. Camii
Eminönü Meydanı
Paşa
Eminönü
124
Şehirhattı İskelesi
Eminönü İskelesi
Sirkeci İskelesi

Hamza Ca
Hacıcılar
Yeni Camii
Sirkeci Feribot İskelesi

10

Küçük
Maçka
Çiftlik Parkı
Parkı

Vişnezade Cad.

E

Taşlık
Parkı

F

Yeniyol Sk.

Babanakkas Baba Efendi

Vişnel Tekke Sk.

I

Ermeni Katolik Sk.
Agop Hastanesi

Hotel
Divan

Hotel
Hyatt
Regency

Taşkışla Cad.

Kadırgalar Cad.

Barbaros Cad.
Barıldım Cad.

Çamlı Köşk

-Kuyular-
caddesi

Cumhuriyet Cad.

Asker Ocağı Cad.

Mete Cad.

Taksim Uluslararası
İş Merkezi

Gazhane Bostanı Sk.

İnönü Stadyumu

Swissôtel
The Bosphorus

Dolmabahçe Cad.

Aydede Cad.

Ceylan
InterContinental

Taksim
Gezi Yeri

Mete Cad.

İstanbul Teknik
Üniversitesi

Miralay Şefik Bey Sk.

Gazhane Caddesi

Dolmabahçe Caddesi

Dolmabahçe
Sarayı

TAKSİM

Taksim
Meydanı

İstanbul Teknik
Üniversitesi

Mühendislik
Fakülteleri

GÜMÜŞSUYU

Dolmabahçe
Saatkulesi

M
Taksim
Abidesi

Cumhuriyet

Tak-ı-
Zafer
Cad.

Gümüşsuyu
Askeri Hastanesi

Osmanlı Sk.

Atatürk
Kültür
Merkezi

Caddesi

Bağ Odaları

Dümen Sk.

Dolmabahçe
Camii

Aya Triada

İnönü

Kazancıbaşı Kazancı Yokuşu

Sıraselviler Cad.

Çifte Vav
Sk.

Çeşme
Sk.

Saray Malçi

Hacı İzzet Paşa Sk.

Çifte Vav
Sk.

Saray Arkası

2

Alman Hast.

Somuncu
Sk.

Kutlu Sk.

Ülker Sk.

Mehmet Selime Hatun Camii Sk.

Molla Bayırı

Mebusan Caddesi

Mecis-i

İnebolu Sokağı

Beşaret Sk.

KABATAŞ

Kabataş

Kabataş

Kabataş Vapur
İskelesi

Kabataş-Beşiktaş

Arslan
Yatağı
Sk.

Cihangir Cad.

Alçak Dam Sk.

Harda Sk.

Deniz
Otobüsü
İskelesi

Kabataş-Üsküdar

3

Doğancı Sk.

Kumrulu Yokuşu

Güneşli Sk.

Emektar Sk.

Cihangir Sk.

Akkavak Sk.

Necatibey Caddesi

Fındıklı Molla
Çelebi Camii

Fındıklı

Susam Sk.

Kumrulu Sk.

Cihangir
Camii

Salıpazarı

Mimar Sinan
Üniversitesi

Eminönü-Beşiktaş

4

İlyas Çelebi Sk.

Enli
Yokuşu

CİHANGİR

Atatürk Kız Lisesi

Caddesi

İstanbul Boğaziçi

5

Antrepolar

kulesi

Karaköy-Kabataş

Modern
zesi

Eyüp-Beyoğlu-Fatih-Eminönü-Üsküdar

önü-Beşiktaş

eci-Harem (Araba Vapurları)

Karaköy-Bakırköy

Karaköy-Haydarpaşa-Kadıköy

200 m

219 yd

6

Kabataş-Adalar-Yalova-Çınarcık

bul-Marmara-Akdeniz Hattı

Saray Burnu

Atatürk
Heykeli

126

Marmara **127** Denizi

200 m
219 yd

A
B
C
123
1
2
3
4
6
Atatürk Köprüsü
Azapkapı Sokullu M. Paşa Camii
ZEYREK
KÜÇÜKPAZAR
Esrar Dede Sk.
Ali Tekin Sk.
Sinan Camii Sk.
Haydar Cad.
Eski İmaret Camii
Eski Mabe Camii
Bıçakçı Çeş. Sk.
Zeyrek Mehmet Paşa Sk.
Fil Yokuşu Sk.
Zeyrek Camii
İbadethane Sk.
Çırçır Cad.
Zeyrek Cad.
Ömer Efendi Sk.
Hüsam Bey Camii
Tezgahcılar Sk.
İtfaiye Cad.
Atatürk Bulvarı
Bostan Hamamı Sk.
Ragıp Gümüşpala Caddesi
Kazancılar Cad.
Küçük Pazar Cad.
İstanbul Ticaret Odası
Sobacılar Caddesi
İst. Manifaturacılar Çarşısı
Hızır Külhanı Sk.
Hacı Kadın Cad.
Şepsefa Hatun Camii
Hoca Gıyasettin Camii
Kepenekçi Sabunhanesi Sk.
Çeşme Cad.
Demirtaş Mescidi
Rüstem Paşa Hamamı
Botanik Enstitüsü
Mimar Sinan Türbesi
Hoca Hamza Mescidi
Sarı Beyazıt Cad.
Şemsettin Sk.
Fetva Yokuşu Sk.
Ord. Prof. Cemil Bilsel Cad.
Hasırcılar
EMİNÖNÜ
Tahtakale Cad.
Azep Askeri Sk.
Vefa Cad.
Kilise Camii
Süleymaniyelmareti Sk.
Süleymaniye Hamamı
Karikatür Müzesi
Resat Nuri Tiyatrosu
Bozdoğan Kemeri
Fatih Belediyesi
Saraçhane Parkı
Kırazlı Camii
Katip Çelebi
Yener Tosyalı Cad.
Şifahane Sk.
Prof. Sıddık Sami Onar Cad.
Süleymaniye Camii
Mimar Sinan Cad.
Siyavuşpaşa Sk.
Uzunçarşı Cad.
Vasıf Çınar
Vefa Lisesi
Molla Hüsrev Camii
Kirazlı Mescit Sk.
Ayşe Kadın Hamamı Sk.
Süleymaniye Cad.
Süleymaniye Kütüphanesi
İstanbul Üniversitesi
Fuat Paşa Caddesi
Örücüler Cad.
Atik İbrahim Paşa Camii
ŞEHZADEBAŞI
Belediye Sarayı
Şehzade Camii
Nevşehirli Damat İb. Paşa Camii
Kalenderhane Camii
Esnaf Hast.
İstanbul Üniversitesi Kütüphanesi
Beyazıt Kulesi
Ali Paşa Camii
Şehzadebaşı Caddesi
Sekbanlar Camii
16 Mart Şehitleri Cad.
İbrahimpaşa Camii
Mercan Cad.
Çakmakçılar Yokuşu
Mercan Ağa Camii
Ahmet Selahattin Sk.
PTT
Hoş Kadem C.
Kemal Paşa Camii
Ağa Yokuşu Sk.
Fevziye Cad.
Vidinli Tevfik Paşa Cad.
Vezneciler Cad.
Bozdoğan Kemeri Cad.
Besim Ömer Paşa Cad.
BEYAZIT
Beyazıt Meydanı
Devlet Kütüphanesi
Çadırcılar Cad.
Yağlıkçılar Cad.
Acıçeşme Sk.
Kapalı Çarşı (Big Bazaar)
Yeşil Tulumba Sk.
Gençtürk Cad.
Mahfil Sk.
Lâleli Camii
Fethibey Cad.
Kurultay Sk.
Harikzedeler Sk.
Büyük Reşit Paşa Cad.
İstanbul Üniversitesi Fen Fakültesi
Üniversite Cad.
Hürriyet Meydanı
Beyazıt Camii
Beyazıt Hamamı
Vakıf Hat Sanatları Müz.
Sahaflar Çarşısı
Hoca Piri Camii
Çorlulu Paşa Camii
Aksaray
Ordu Caddesi
Lâleli-Üniversite
Yeniçeriler Caddesi
Beyazıt
Atik Paşa Camii
Sait Efendi Sk.
Şair Haşmet Sk.
Koca Ragıp Kütüpha nesi
Sekban Yakup Ağa Camii
Soğan Ağa Camii Sk.
Bodrum Camii
Mithatpaşa Cad.
Tiyatro Cad.
Y. Kemal Müzesi
Mesih Paşa Cad.
NİŞANCA
Lâleli Cad.
Tatlı Kuyu Hamamı Sk.
Gedik Paşa Camii
Azimkar Sk.
Daltaban Yok. Sk.
Tavşantaşı Sk.
Turanlı Sk.
Katip Sinan Camii
Esir Kemal Camii
Emin Sinan Hamamı Sk.
Mustafa Kemal Caddesi
Hayriye Tüccarı Cad.
Nişanca Bostan Sk.
İbrahim Paşa Yok.
Türkeli Cad.
Niş. Mehmet Paşa Camii
Muhsine Hatun Camii
Gedikpaşa Cad.
Tülcü Sk.
Katip Kasım Camii Sk.
Güvenlik Cad.
Asya Sk.
Türkeli Çıkmazı
KUMKAPI
Bali Paşa Yok.
Katip Kasım Camii
Molla-taşı Cad.
İsmail Sefa Sk.
Hemşehri Sk.
Kenan Bey Sk.
Mollataşı Cad.
Çifte Gelinler Cad.
C. Ahmet Camii
Kadırga Limanı Cad.
Neviye
Alişan Sk.
Nalbant Camii
Şarapnel Sk.
Tavaşi Çeşme Sk.
Ördekli Bakkal Sk.
Kumkapı Meydanı
Kumluk Sk.
Şair Sermet Sk.
Işıl Sk.
YENİKAPI
Kennedy (Sahil Yolu) Caddesi
Kumkapı İst. Cad.
Kumkapı İstasyonu
Yenıkapı Denız Otobüs İskelesi
Feribot İskelesi
Yenikapı-Bostancı Yenikapı-Moda
Yenikapı-Bakırköy
Marmara Deniz

GALATA
Arap
Cami
Kemer
Necatibey
Mumhane Cad.
F
Bankalar Cad.
SALT
St. George Hast.
Kemankes Cad.
124
Pazari Kapi
Zindan Han Sk.
Bilur Sk.
Perçemli Sk.
Tersane Cad.
Karaköy
Karaköy
Denizcilik İşletmeleri Müdürlüğü
KARAKÖY
İstanbul Boğaziçi
1
Fermeneciler Cad.
Kurekcüler Kapisi Sk.
Karaköy Meyd.
Yeralti Camii
Kemankes Must. Pş. Camii
Deniz Otobüsü İskelesi
Rihtim Cad.
Karaköy Vapur İskelesi
Karaköy-Kabataş
Galata Köprüsü

Eminönü-Beşiktaş
Eyüp-Beyoğlu-Fatih-Eminönü-Üsküdar

Sirkeci-Harem (Araba Vapurları)
Karaköy-Haydarpaşa-Kadıköy
İstanbul-Marmara-Akdeniz Hattı

Eminönü Meydani
10
Şehirhatti İskelesi
Saray Burnu
Atatürk Heykeli
2
İnönü
Reşadiye Caddesi
Eminönü İskelesi
Sirkeci İskelesi
Yeni Camii
Arpacilar Camii
Yali Köşkü Cad.
SİRKECİ
Sirkeci Feribot İskelesi
Kennedy (Sahil Yolu) Caddesi
Daye Hatun Mescidi
Hatice Turhan
Mimar Kemalettin
Sirkeci İstasyon Cad.
Gotlar Sütunu
3
S. Türbesi
S. Hâmit Türbesi
Büyük Postane Cad.
Hamidiye Cad.
Borsa
Sirkeci Garı
İstasyon Arkası Sk.
Nöbethane Cad.
Gülhane
Tanzimat Müzesi
Âşir Efendi Cad.
Ankara Caddesi
Ebussuud Cad.
Hüdavendigar Cad.
İbni Kemal Cad.
Karaki Hüs. Çelebi Camii
Parkı
Eski Şark Eserleri Müzesi
Çinili Köşkü
Topkapı Sarayı Müzesi
4
Bâb-üs Selâm
OĞLU
Cemal Nadir Sk.
PTT
İstanbul Erek Lisesi
Bâb-ı Âli Camii
Gülhane
İstanbul Vilayet
Hükümet Konağı Cad.
Bâb-ı Âli Cad.
Alay Köşki
Arkeoloji Müzesi
Konstantin Suru
Mektebi Sk.
Türkocağı Cad.
Çağaloğlu Hamamı
Ağa Camii
Aya İrini Kilise Müzesi
Bâb-i Hümayun
Ahmet III Çeşmesi
Mahmutpaşa Camii
SULTANAHMET
Molla Fenari Camii
Yerebatan Camii
Söğükçeşme Sk.
Alemdar Cad.
Nuruosmaniye Gazi Cad.
Bâb-ı Âli Caddesi
Alibaba
Yerebatan Cad.
Yerebatan Sarayı
5
Hagia Sophia (Ayasofya C. Müz.)
İshak Paşa
Çatal Çeşme Sk.
emberlitaş amamı
Basın Müzesi
Sultanahmet
Soğuk Müzesi
Ayasofya Meydani
Babıhümayun Cad.
Caddesi
Divanyolu Cad.
Binbirdirek Sarnıcı
Ölçek Cad.
Sultan-ahmet Parkı
Haseki Ham.
İshak Paşa Camii
Ahırkapı Feneri
5
Köprülü Küt.
Klodfarer Cad.
Alman Çeşmesi
Ayasofya Meydani
Mimar Mehmet Aga Cad.
Derive Tenasül Hastalıkları Hastanesi
Dirdariye Sok.
Terzihane Sk.
Türk ve İslam Eserleri Müz.
Dikilitaş
Vakıflar Halı Müzesi
Ucandere
Yerbiyik Sk.
Cankurtaran İstasyonu
2
Ücler Sk.
Atmeydani
Örme Sütun
Mimar Mehmet Aga Cad.
Akbıyık Cad.
Cankurtaran İlkokulu
ehmet aşa C.
SK.
Tavukhane Sk.
Yılan Sütun
Sultan Ahmet Camii
Kabasakal Cad.
Torun Sk.
Yeni Akbıyık Cad.
Mozaik Müzesi
Cankurtaran Hakkı Sk.
Kaleci Cad.
Nakilbent Sk.
Küçük Ayasofya Cad.
Aksakal Sk.
Nakilbent Camii
Aksakal Sk.
Akbıyık Değirmeni Sk.
Fenerli Kapı Sk.
Keresteci Hakkı Sk.
Ahır Kapı Sk.
ya Camii
Üçük Ayasofya Camii
ÇATLADIKAPI
Oyuncu Sk.
Kennedy (Sahil Yolu) Caddesi
Yenikapı-Harem

200 m
219 yd

129

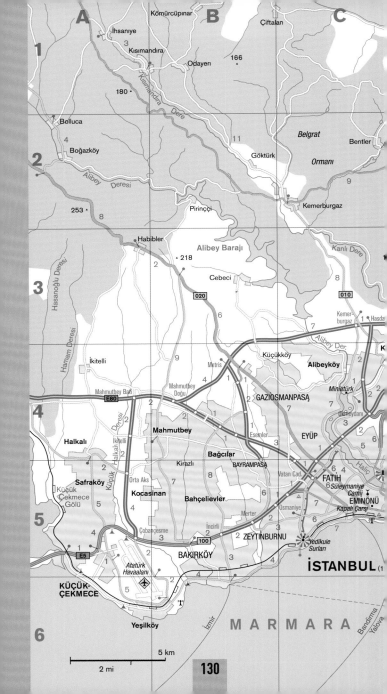

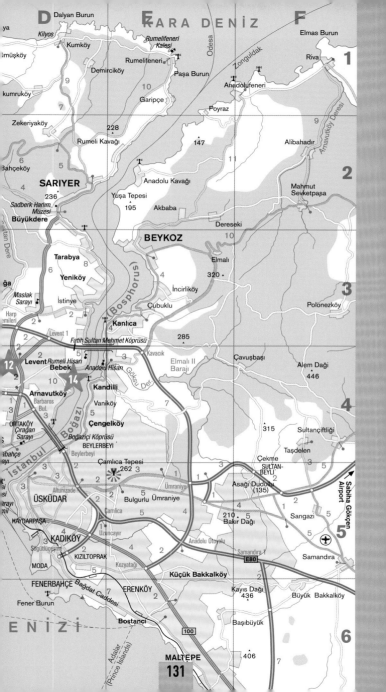

This index lists a selection of the streets and squares shown in the street atlas

STREET INDEX

STREET INDEX

KEY TO STREET ATLAS

𝗠̂	Museum
🎭	Stage / Bühne
🛈	Information
☪	Mosque / Moschee
✝	Church / Kirche
✡	Synagogue / Synagoge
☾	Hospital / Krankenhaus
✶	Police / Polizei
✉	Post
📖	Library / Bibliothek
𝗜	Monument / Denkmal
⌂	Hammam / Türkisches Bad
🅿 🅿	Parking / Parkhaus /-platz
──●──	Tram with stop / Tram mit Haltestelle
──M──	Metro with station / U-Bahn mit Bahnhof
─────·	Metro under construction / U-Bahn in Bau
── ── ──	Fähre
▢	Remarkable building / Bemerkenswertes Gebäude
▢	Public building / Öffentliches Gebäude
▢	Green / Grünfläche
▢	Uncovered area / Unbebaute Fläche
⁄⁄⁄⁄⁄	Pedestrian zone / Fußgängerzone
▬▬▬	Walking tours / Stadtspaziergänge
⭐1	MARCO POLO Highlight

INDEX

This index lists all sights, museums and destinations plus the main squares and streets, the key terms and people featured in this guide. Numbers in bold indicate a main entry.

CREDITS

WRITE TO US

e-mail: info@marcopologuides.co.uk

Did you have a great holiday?
Is there something on your mind?
Whatever it is, let us know!
Whether you want to praise, alert us to errors or give us a personal tip – MARCO POLO would be pleased to hear from you.
We do everything we can to provide the very latest information for your trip.

Nevertheless, despite all of our authors' thorough research, errors can creep in. MARCO POLO does not accept any liability for this. Please contact us by e-mail or post.

MARCO POLO Travel Publishing Ltd
Pinewood, Chineham Business Park
Crockford Lane, Chineham
Basingstoke, Hampshire RG24 8AL
United Kingdom

PICTURE CREDITS
Cover Photograph: Look: age fotostock (Ortaköy Mosque, Fatih-Sultan-Mehmet-Bridge)
Images: Selim Baklacı (16 centre); R. Hackenberg (flap l., flap r., 9, 24 l., 33 top, 38, 44/45, 56, 58, 59, 65, 70, 101, 102/103, 103, 104, 108 bottom, 115); Huber: Schmid (2 top, 5, 10/11, 55), Serrano (8); Hush Hostel Lounge: Hikmet Tanur (16 top); Laif: Butzmann (94), Kimmig (51), Perkovic (22), Siemers (3 Mi., 80/81), Tophoven (79), Türemis (48, 62, 82, 85, 105); Laif/narphotos: Serra Akcan (25); Laif/Onlocation: Keribar: (104/105); Look: Pompe (86), Zegers (40); mauritius images: AGE (68 r.), Alamy (2 centre top, 6), Bibikow (66), Kord (7); D. Renckhoff (2 centre bottom, 3 top, 3 bottom, 21, 24 r., 26/27, 30, 32/33, 41, 46, 68 l., 72/73, 76, 88/89, 96/97, 99, 100, 108 top, 109); santralistanbul (16 bottom); T. Stankiewicz (2 bottom, 4, 12/13, 15, 35, 36/37, 49, 53, 60/61, 74, 90, 102, 120/121,); J. Stumpe (18/19, 93); Sumahan: Mr.Koray Erkaya (17 top); Ahmet Tozar (17 bottom); D. Zaptçıoğlu/J. Gottschlich (1 bottom)

1st Edition 2012
Worldwide Distribution: Marco Polo Travel Publishing Ltd, Pinewood, Chineham Business Park, Crockford Lane, Basingstoke, Hampshire RG24 8AL, United Kingdom. Email: sales@marcopolouk.com
© MAIRDUMONT GmbH & Co. KG, Ostfildern
Chief editors: Michaela Lienemann (concept, managing editor), Marion Zorn (concept, text editor)
Author: Dilek Zaptçıoğlu, Jürgen Gottschlich; Editor: Felix Wolf
Programme supervision: Anita Dahlinger, Ann-Katrin Kutzner, Nikolai Michaelis
Picture editor: Barbara Schmid, Gabriele Forst
What's hot: wunder media, München
Cartography of street atlas: DuMont Reisekartografie, Fürstenfeldbruck, © MAIRDUMONT, Ostfildern
Cartography pull-out map: DuMont Reisekartografie, Fürstenfeldbruck, © MAIRDUMONT, Ostfildern
Design: milchhof: atelier, Berlin; Front cover, pull-out map cover, page 1: factor product munich
Translated from German by John Sykes, Cologne; editor of the English edition: Kathleen Becker, Lisbon
Prepress: BW-Medien GmbH, Leonberg
Phrase book in cooperation with Ernst Klett Sprachen GmbH, Stuttgart, Editorial by Pons Wörterbücher

DOS & DON'TS 👆

A few things you should watch out for in İstanbul

HIGH SPIRITS? BEWARE...

As the rate of VAT is high, illegal distilling is on the rise in Turkey. Even though the government is taking firm measures to stop this, fatal cases of methyl alcohol poisoning are a common occurrence. This is largely a result of drinking spirits such as vodka, gin and rakı. In respectable cafés and restaurants you can rely on the genuineness of the drinks, but don't go boozing in dubious-looking bars in the back streets. It's also advisable not to buy alcoholic drinks from kiosks, and if you do drink anything bought there, don't do so alone in your hotel room. If you suspect you have alcohol poisoning, make your way to the nearest hospital without delay!

DISPLAYING AFFECTION IN PUBLIC

Public displays of affection between lovers are frowned upon in Turkey. This is considered to be bad behaviour at the very least, and may result in disapproving looks or a verbal reproach. Sex is still generally a taboo subject in Turkey. So even if the romantic atmosphere of İstanbul takes hold of you – keep the kisses for the hotel room!

KEEP AN EYE ON YOUR WALLET

Petty crime has increased in İstanbul in recent years. Watch out for pickpockets, who are most active in Sultanahmet, at the bazaars and in Beyoğlu, because they regard tourists as easy prey. Keep a firm grip on your bag! Don't let anyone persuade you to go with them to bars or dance clubs that you don't know – you might wake up the next morning with a throbbing headache and without your wallet.

FALLING FOR TOUTS AND CONFIDENCE TRICKSTERS

You only need to pay one visit to the Grand Bazaar or stroll through the park in front of the Blue Mosque to make the acquaintance of the *korsan* (pirates). Usually you will be approached in front of a shop or bar and informed all about the supposed attractions of the establishment. These tactics are obvious, but there are also touts who pose as helpers and tell you about a brother who runs a shop where the carpets are especially cheap or a hotel that you really must take a look at. The best policy is to ignore these people.

PICKING UP STONES

For some years Turkish customs officers have meticulously monitored the export of items that might be regarded as artistic or cultural treasures, as in previous decades the country was robbed of antiquities by smugglers. There is a risk therefore that stones or fossils picked up in all innocence will be confiscated by Customs and heavy fines slapped on the owners. So it's wise not to put any old-looking stones or fossils in your baggage!